Natural Palettes

Natural
Palettes

—

Inspiration
from
Plant-Based
Color

Sasha Duerr

Princeton Architectural Press · New York

For my Aunt Kathleen, believer in beauty,
heart of gold, lover of plants, supporter of dreams.
For Kara, who deeply loved both the garden
and the woods with me. And for my grandmothers:
these rainbows are for you…

Contents

Introduction

Plants are indelible storytellers, connecting us emotionally, physically, environmentally. A walk in the woods, the remains of a summer meal, the scent of California sagebrush, a June bouquet—all provide depths of inspiration from which we draw meaning. At the same time, the very plants that make these moments often produce vivid natural colors that tell *color stories* rooted in authentic experiences and relationships.

Working with plant-based palettes can make us aware of seasonal availability and growth cycles as well as the biodiversity of the world around us. In the food world, *terroir* means much more than merely the circumstances that create a better-tasting grape; in the world of natural color it is by knowing our sources that we can begin to appreciate the process, grasp its meaning, and most fully participate.

This is strikingly different from the fast-fashion and design industries, where every year sees the release of "hot" new "it" colors promoted by flashy marketing campaigns that hook the consumer on synthetic ingredients and rapid production cycles. Living Coral, Pantone's 2019 Color of the Year, will have shown up everywhere, in products sold in fast-fashion and home-goods store aisles, later to be discounted and then discarded, often to end in landfills—or worse. Ultimately its chemical dyes will seep back into our oceans, likely only further bleaching out the coral for which the color was far too ironically named. With fast fashion, as with fast food, there's little emphasis on the environmental fallout from production or the negative social impacts of rapid corporate overproduction. Rivers are drenched in the chemical residues of last season's colors and landfills continue to pile up and exponentially overflow, yet all the while we're encouraged to go out to buy something—anything—new.

While fast-fashion seasons move quickly and relentlessly, practices based in natural palettes can slow down the pace of our lives and reconnect us to true living hues, actual organic plant-based ingredients, real seasonality, and, above all else, natural limits.

Working professionally with plant-based color for the past twenty years, through research, experimentation, and collaborations, has helped me to rethink our society's patterns of color and consumption. In 2007, with the help of my dear friend and colleague Katelyn Toth-Fejel, I founded the organization Permacouture Institute as a way to explore regenerative design practices for fashion and textiles.

Using natural color as a conduit between slow food and slow fashion, we created a series called Dinners to Dye For in collaboration with slow-food chefs. Bringing communities together for a seasonal meal—and using the by-products and food waste from its preparation to make color—provided the occasion for exploring the potential of vibrant color palettes, redefining the way we conceive of waste, and appreciating the value of socially connecting and engaging our senses. Another series, Weed Your Wardrobe, is held in community gardens when people gather to give their unwanted clothing and textiles a fresh new life. They weed the garden, create dyes from those same abundant weeds, and refresh their items with the dyes made, all while questioning what is valuable and desirable.

These are but two small examples of a much larger, ongoing coevolution of the food, fashion, and design worlds and their increasing collective turn toward plants as an enduring source of inspiration and collaboration. Within this context, I believe plant-based color will only continue to evolve and to influence generations to come—as it has for generations before.

Exploring local and seasonal plant-made palettes has become for me a form of art and design thinking. Cultivating connections through the creation of plant-based color from food and floral waste as well as from medicinal and otherwise beneficial plants can be regenerative to our ecosystems and nourishing to our relationships and our communities. To me there is no comparison to the beauty of the true hues that emerge.

PLANT PALETTES

I love the process of working with plant-based palettes as much as the end product. Creating plant-made color is similar to and can even be symbiotic with cooking; they share the same steps of choosing from a multitude of recipes and methods, finding the right ingredients and tools, experimenting with techniques, and refining timing. Just as a chef's knowledge of local and seasonal ingredients might influence a menu, an awareness of the stages through which chosen plants ripen, are harvestable, and even vary from year to year makes a difference in the creation of hues.

It is essential to understand the pros and cons of natural color and to design with each plant's unique characteristics in mind. When working with living ingredients, when and where the plants are harvested, the alchemy of the soil, the pH of the water, how much rain and sun a plant receives, and the timing and application of the natural color-making process all play a part in the shades, depths, and range of hues created.

One of the many advantages of working with plant-based colors is that often multiple parts of one species of plant can be used to create a whole new spectrum of hues. For instance, balsam branches can yield a range of cool yellows, inky blues, and dark grays, while the cones will yield warm tones, blushing pinks, and dusty mauves. Using just the flowers, leaves, or roots of a dandelion can conjure individual colors as well. Plant-made palettes are the essence of time and place and are enhanced by your own openness to the process— as well as the patience and practice it requires to embrace color on nature's timing.

Working with various types of materials and fibers can create a full range of different shades from the same dye bath. A plant-based color often can be shifted easily by using a mordant (a plant-based or metallic binder that can change dye colors as well as stabilize them to have more light- and washfastness) or by altering the pH of the dye bath through the introduction of some other modifier, typically an acid or a base. Many plants, such as acorns, avocado pits, loquat leaves, and pomegranate rinds, contain tannins that are excellent mordants on their own.

When I use metallic mordants, I work with the minimum amounts needed for a successful result, and I use only alum (aluminum sulfate for protein fibers and aluminum acetate for cellulose fibers) and iron salts (ferrous sulfate, which works for both protein and cellulose fibers), since those are considered the safest. Other metallic mordants such as copper, tin, and chrome are suggested in old natural dye books—as well as in a few recent ones! These heavy-metal mordants are toxic and should be avoided. A rule of thumb: just because it is natural doesn't mean it's good for you. Always use common sense and do your homework.

However, even alum and iron salts should be treated with caution, as they can be irritants and, in the case of iron, toxic if accidentally ingested in larger doses, especially to small children and pets. With awareness and proper precautions—gloves, lids on pots, dust masks—you can work with these materials safely and efficiently.

I work with 8 percent of the weight of the dry natural fiber for alum salts and 2 to 4 percent of the weight of the dry natural fiber for iron salts. To save energy and to prevent unnecessary exposure to fumes from steam, I often use cold processing for pre-mordanting (alum) before adding materials to a dye bath and post-mordanting (iron), where you can add your predyed fibers to shift or change the color. I like working with nonreactive stainless steel pots; it is simple to add exactly measured ingredients, and they are easily cleaned. But if you want to work more experimentally, you can use aluminum or iron pots as an alternative to adding their metallic salts.

Plant-made colors can easily be overdyed and shifted throughout the lifetime of a garment, textile, or decor. Dyeing a dress bright yellow with goldenrod flowers, for example, could allow you at any point to shift the color to a dark, rich green or to add a pattern with just a dip in iron water. This permits you to modularly work with your evolving style and color choices while personalizing your wardrobe with your favorite plants or the by-products of a meaningful experience—say, the leftovers of a special bouquet! This emotional and environmental connection helps us to want to care for it and to extend its life and life cycle.

Just as we extract flavors in cooking, you can extract natural colors through a variety of processes. Bringing plants to a boil, then to a low simmer, then steeping until the desired shade is reached is one way a color can be extracted, but there are many techniques that can conjure deep and satisfying plant-based palettes. Working with cold-dye processes, where time does the work of soaking and steeping your ingredients, is one low-impact and climate-friendly approach. There are also ways to carefully cultivate fermentation processes (as with organic indigo or with green persimmon fruit) over time and without heat. Heating and extracting through solar processes is another satisfying way to create color. I often steep plants in large glass jars with passive and elemental help from the sun's energy. You can also steam color-producing plants directly on your materials, saving water and often creating deeper, more direct hues.

Other ecologically engaged strategies include collecting rainwater instead of using municipal sources, experimenting with saltwater as a naturally abundant resource, using leftover dye baths to their very last drop, and working with plants that can provide "compost tea" to add to your garden instead of producing wastewater— for example, comfrey leaves, which deliver a soil nutrient for healthy apple trees. Planting low-water, drought-tolerant color-producing plants in your garden is one more way to reduce your consumption of resources. And color made from common weeds or floral and food waste can be an accessible and very direct way of giving your decor, wardrobe, woodwork, or even art processes a dynamic new life.

How we care for our textiles can account for 75 to 80 percent of their lifetime carbon footprint. I often find that the success of a hue relies upon how we engage with it. Instead of throwing a naturally dyed T-shirt in the wash on high heat with harsh detergents and then in the dryer on high heat, I choose a gentle, pH-neutral soap, cold washing, and drying naturally—easier on the planet as well as on natural colors and fibers!

Plant-based color generally binds well to protein-based fibers (animal-based fibers like silk and wool). These materials can be organic and compostable. By their very nature they require delicate care—hand washing and line or flat drying. Refreshing an old wool sweater with a gorgeous, plant-made hue that naturally resists moths, like lavender, or disinfects, like green tea, is another way to extend the life cycle of a textile.

The palette swatches in this book were all created on the same material: silk. Known as a "universal receptor," it accepts a wide range of natural color. Other materials might take the same color very differently, and sometimes better, just as measurements and timing can change the outcome of a recipe. When I test a plant's color potential, I love to create swatches in a wide range of fibers and materials to access a full range of hues.

In addition to my previous books, which have many seasonal color recipes, the list of curated resources at the back of this book will help you to get started or to deepen your practice. With patience and openness, you can evolve your own art and craft of creating natural hues, just as with cooking—throughout a lifetime, with every new season, ingredient, and alchemy of time and place. I have come to realize that, just like the uniqueness and biodiversity of living colors themselves, there is no singular model for a successful practice with plant-based color—so much depends on your design purpose, ingredients, and engagement. You can be experimental; you can follow recipes. As you learn, remain open, record your successes, and remember that you can be guided through your senses.

Below is a key indicating what was added to create the natural colors throughout this book:

PLANT PALETTE COLOR KEY

—

NM = No additional mordant added
Al = Alum (aluminum sulfate)
FE = Iron (ferrous sulfate)
AL+FE = Alum (aluminum sulfate) + iron (ferrous sulfate)

KNOWING YOUR INGREDIENTS:
PLANT IDENTIFICATION

—

Working from scratch using plant ingredients requires a knowledge of plant types and species to ensure you are not mistaking, say, poison hemlock for Queen Anne's lace. Plants are powerful. Properly researching their qualities and being aware of your own body's interaction with them (personal allergies, et cetera) are central to cultivating a healthy practice.

Common Name: The everyday name we use to refer to a plant. Common names can vary depending on region and culture.

Botanical Name: The botanical name of a plant is important for positive and proper identification and classification. Botanical names are a standardized system that can be used uniformly throughout the world.

Plant Description: Each plant variety featured in the palettes includes a description. Knowing the ecologies and everyday uses of plants can deepen our knowledge of how to work and care for them.

Understanding the depth and variety of a plant's potential can be both practically and conceptually helpful in creating or choosing healthy, meaningful, and connected natural palettes. In addition, knowing about each plant from an ethnobotanical perspective helps to further our understanding of its important cultural, medicinal, and culinary uses, its connection to indigenous people and practices, and its deep role in nourishing the diversity of ecologies, communities, and their rhythms.

Plant palettes can help us become aware of—and even to become stewards of—the natural world. A brilliant spectrum of hues can be found in places we may never have expected: beautiful colors from the by-products and compost of a dinner with friends, a rainbow from the weeds you pass by every day, color therapy in sync with healing hues, or a palette created from pruning the branches of your favorite backyard fruit trees. These plant-based hues create holistic color systems and provide endless inspiration—designed by nature and ready for our active participation.

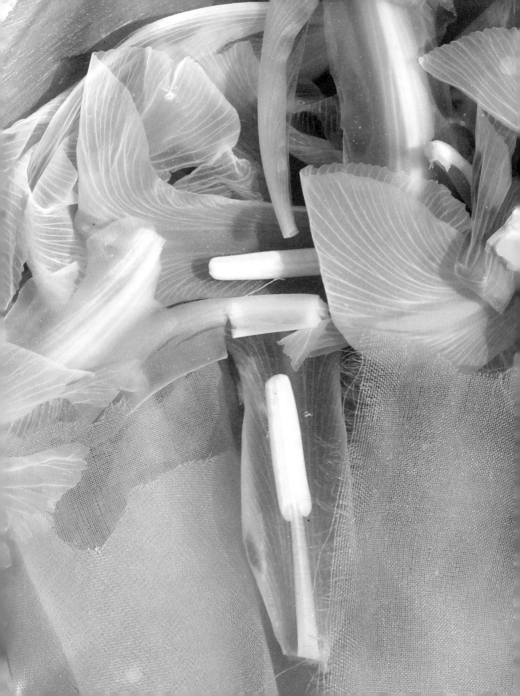

Living Color

Colors from living sources come in a vital
spectrum of tones that have a unique ability
to organically harmonize with one another. From
a sensory perspective, plants provide the perfect
natural color palettes to soothe us or to bring
energy to any project, delivering a range of
shades that can represent a multiplicity of ideas.

With natural color, you can achieve spectra of
hues that are difficult or perhaps even impossible
to produce synthetically. Even grays can hold
a rainbow of tones. Natural colors are never flat
but change in different lights and respond to
shifting environments. In contrast to one-note
synthetic colors squeezed directly out of a tube,
these colors are dynamic, unique, and alive.

Another characteristic of natural color is
what I call "imbued hue." Natural colors may at
first appear very pale or even neutral, but they
possess a glow that pulls your attention from the
other side of the room like the light reflected
off a luna moth's wings. An energy exists in the

natural color molecules of these "neutral neons" that inspires literal and poetic shifts in the way we view color and color theory itself.

Witnessing and documenting the diversity of living palettes has made me more sensitive to color—both in the environment and in my own art and design practice. The biodiversity of these true hues from natural sources and the specific alchemy and uniqueness of living color have become my life's work. I've learned that just as biodiversity plays a crucial role in food through creating a spectrum of flavor that is essential to nutrition and evolution, biodiversity has an equally crucial role in creating harmonious hues that color our perception of the world.

1 GOOD THINGS COME IN TREES

Eucalyptus Leaves   Willow Branches   Osage Orange Wood

Leaves, branches, prunings, wood chips, and even sawdust from a wide range of tree species can make beautiful colors. The lumber, woodworking, and arborist industries can all provide the necessary raw materials to craft these wood-based colorways. Here are just a few examples of trees that can produce tremendous color tones.

Elm Branches   Alder Branches

Eucalyptus Leaves

Eucalyptus

Eucalyptus is a fast-growing, mostly evergreen tree. The name is derived from the Greek, meaning "well covered." There are over seven hundred varieties of eucalyptus; most are native to Australia, including the world's tallest flowering trees. All parts of the eucalyptus can make dyes that are substantive, meaning that they require no mordant. Eucalyptus works especially well on silk, wool, and other protein fibers. Depending on the type of eucalyptus, you may discover different shades and tones of deep rust-red, coral, oranges, yellows, green, and dark brown that can be produced from their leaves.

1 NM	2 AL
3 AL+FE	4 FE

Willow Branches

—

Salix

There are around four hundred species of willow;
most are found in the Northern Hemisphere, in moist
soil. Both the leaves and the bark of willow trees are
natural remedies to relieve headaches and other pain
and have been used to this purpose for centuries.
The branches and bark of this tree, with its cascading
leaves and rustling beauty, also provide soothing
shades of soft pink, green, and gray.

1 NM	2 AL
3 AL+FE	4 FE

Osage Orange Wood

—

Maclura pomifera

Osage orange is a tree native to a small area of
the United States, encompassing eastern Texas,
southeastern Oklahoma, and southwestern Arkansas.
The tree is named for the Osage Nation, which is
located in this region. Osage orange bears large fruit
that is inedible even to birds and other wildlife.
Sawdust from the Osage orange, also known as the
hedge apple tree, creates clear yellows, oranges,
and greens.

1 NM	2 AL
3 AL+FE	4 FE

Elm Branches

—

Ulmus

Elms are deciduous and semi-deciduous trees that once played a significant role in mixed forests. Unfortunately, in the modern era, Dutch elm disease, caused by a beetle and a parasitic fungus, has eliminated many elms. This is tragic ecologically and also culturally, as elms have long been prized for their strength and resistance to splitting, among other properties. Fortunately, cultivars of elm with fungal resistance have now been developed, and elms are well on their way toward restoration. Prunings from elm trees and bark from felled trees can make beautiful colors, from pinks and corals to deep mauves and gray-greens.

1	2
NM	AL
3	4
AL+FE	FE

Alder Branches

—

Alnus species

Alder is readily found in the wild in North America, making it an easy tree to forage from; it can be helpful at times to thin out alders in forests where they've become ecologically over-expressed. Native American cultures used red alder bark to treat skin irritations, poison oak, and insect bites. Alders love to grow near rivers, streams, and wetlands. The wood of the alder is often used in making furniture and cabinetry. Alder can create hues of light pink, rich green, and dark ocher-green.

1 NM	2 AL
3 AL+FE	4 FE

2   COLOR BLOOMS

Black Hollyhock Flowers   Common Sunflower   Dahlia Flowers

Hot pinks from safflower petals, teal blues from
black hollyhocks, and bright oranges from marigolds—
together these blooming beauties can add unexpectedly
gorgeous hues to any home or wardrobe. Beginning
their life in the joyful form of a bouquet, the blooms of
this petal palette later reemerged as the raw ingredients
for future creativity. Its flower-powered tones offer
an inspiring way to reuse common waste products from
the floral industry or spent bouquets from weddings
and other festivities as well as a means to produce the
most local colors of all: those made from the blooms
in your very own flower garden.

Marigold Flowers   Safflower   Purple Iris Flowers

Black Hollyhock Flowers

—

Alcea rosea 'Nigra'

Hollyhocks are typically towering plants with big, beautiful blooms; black hollyhocks have velvety, colorful petals. Quite breathtaking in the garden, the flowers of these heritage perennials are easy to collect and to use for making natural color. Hollyhock hues range in depth from lavender to purples, teal blues, and gorgeous dark greens.

1 NM	2 AL
3 AL+FE	4 FE

Common Sunflower

—

Helianthus annuus

Sunflowers may have first been domesticated as long ago as 2600 BCE in Mexico as well as in the American South and Southwest. The flower is an inflorescence, meaning that the center is made up of hundreds of tiny flowers. Honeybees and bumblebees are two of the most common pollinators, with bumblebees being especially important for the sunflower's success. All parts of the plant, from the flowerheads to the stock and leaves, produce a range of shades, depending on the variety. Common yellow sunflower heads create grayish yellows, grayish greens, and deeper shades of teal gray.

1 NM	2 AL
3 AL+FE	4 FE

Dahlia Flowers

—

Dahlia

An herbaceous perennial native to Central America,
the dahlia is a showstopper in the floral world. The Aztecs
grew the tubers as a valued food crop, and dahlias were
declared the national flower of Mexico in 1963. Today,
the dahlia is still considered a staple ingredient in Oaxacan
cuisine. The dahlia's showy and colorful blooms attract
pollinators through the shape and color of their petals
rather than their scent. There are more than fifty-seven
thousand dahlia cultivars. Dahlias are annual bloomers
and are stunning additions to floral arrangements. Dyes
made from dahlias range in hue from yellows to oranges
to light and dark greens.

1 NM	2 AL
3 AL+FE	4 FE

Marigold Flowers

—

Tagetes

Well loved around the world, marigolds enjoy extensive use in celebrations, festivals, and spiritual and religious rituals, especially in Mexico, India, Nepal, and Thailand. The marigold's glowing orange, red, and yellow flowers add beauty and bring beneficial bugs to the garden. They make excellent cut flowers and are gorgeous in garlands. The marigold is a wonderful, stable, and rich dye source; the flowers' heads produce golden yellows and oranges and deep greens and olives, too.

1 NM	2 AL
3 AL+FE	4 FE

Safflower

—

Carthamus tinctorius

Safflower, an annual in the thistle family, is one of the world's oldest crops. Safflower has been traditionally grown for its oil and seeds and to make flavorings and medicine. Used as a dye, safflowers have even been traced back to King Tutankhamun's tomb in ancient Egypt. The safflower is known as *benibana* in Japan. The Japanese have mastered the fine art of extracting the pink and red color from its petals—a process known as *benimochi*—as 99 percent of the flower contains a yellow pigment that must be boiled out; the remaining 1 percent produces these awe-inspiring bright pinks. Dried safflower petals are a known source of carthamin, also known as carthamus red or natural red, which has amazing capabilities to produce red, yellow, and bright pink dyes.

1 NM	2 AL
3 AL+FE	4 FE

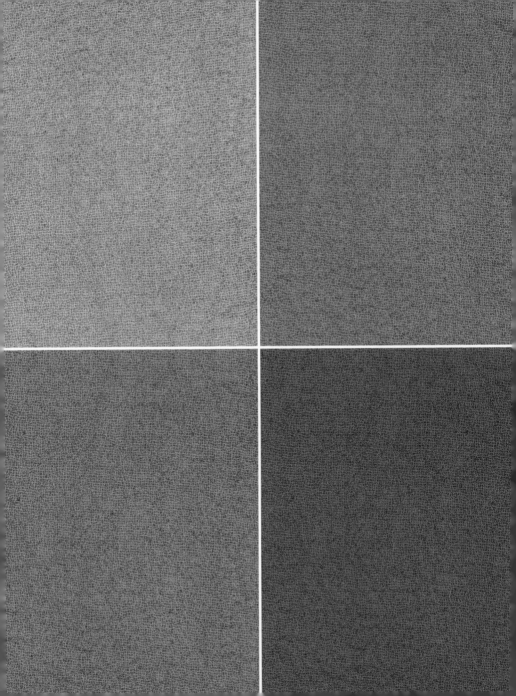

Purple Iris Flowers

Iris

Irises, with their ethereal blue and purple petals, can have different color properties depending on which part of the plant is used. The iris takes its name from the Greek word for "rainbow," which is also the name of the Greek goddess of the rainbow. It is a perennial grown from creeping rhizome roots; the genus comprises nearly three hundred species. Purple and blue iris petals yield shades of light lavenders, gray blues, and rich beiges.

1 NM	2 AL
3 AL+FE	4 FE

3 ROSE-COLORED GLASSES

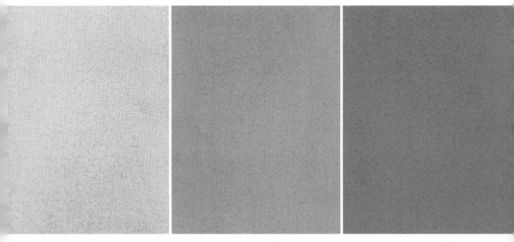

Red Rose Petals   Red Rose Petals   Red Rose Petals

Roses are enjoyed for their ornamental beauty in cut bouquets, as culinary ingredients, and in perfumes, medicines, and beauty products. Once the plant has fruited and produced rose hips, they can be used to make a healing tea that is very high in vitamin C. They also provide a rich source of the chemical binders called tannins. Rose petals of all shades can provide unsurpassed beauty in pinks, lilacs, violets, and blacks, and rose leaves and stems can create tans, light greens, deep greens, and blacks.

Rose Leaves and Stems   Rose Leaves and Stems   Rose Hips

Red Rose Petals

—

Rosa

There are over three hundred varieties and thousands of cultivars of roses. Dark red, pink, and purple roses provide the deepest natural colors. The red rose is extremely popular as a symbol of love, both in the garden and in the floral industry. After these flowers have been enjoyed on Valentine's Day or any special occasion, before they have been thrown out or sent to the green waste bin, a wonderful opportunity arises to make beautiful colors. Organic flowers are always best when making natural color. Roses are pH sensitive, and dark red and purple rose petals can create pink, fuchsia, purple, blue, or black dye, depending on the pH modifiers used.

1 NM	2 AL
3 AL+FE	4 FE

Rose Leaves and Stems

—

Rosa

Roses developed thorns most likely to protect themselves
and to keep their roots firmly planted. The stems and leaves
of roses are often considered less for alternative usages
than rose petals in both bouquets and the home garden.
After a bouquet is spent, the green stems and leaves will
often linger on for some time. Pruning the roses in one's
own flower garden is essential; their green waste clippings
create beautiful tans, greens, grays, and blacks.

1 NM	2 AL
3 AL+FE	4 FE

Rose Hips

—

Rosa

The fruit of the rose is a berrylike structure called a rose hip. Rose hips are the result of successful pollination of the rose flower in the spring or early summer; they develop in late summer or early fall. Rose hips are loaded with vitamin C and have many culinary and medicinal uses. They can be used to make tea, jam, jelly, marmalade, and even wine. Their colors are warm sandy tans, moody grays, and blacks.

1 NM	2 AL
3 AL+FE	4 FE

Deepening Our
Color Senses

I fell in love with natural color by making it—
through the sensory aspects of connecting to
a color from its origin, caring for it, and seeing
the hidden beauty in wayward weeds, discarded
peels, or prunings from my own backyard.
I also fell in love with the immersive process—
the magic of making pinks and mauves from
slowly simmering sweet gum leaves just collected
from a storm and, when on the stove, smelling
like nutmeg in a November rain.

Plant palettes can originate from our most
authentic experiences of the natural world.
From the ingredients gathered to the hues
created, the practice of working with plant-
made colors fully engages our senses while also
providing opportunities to become more aware
and engaged with our ecologies. And, as with
other regenerative design practices, we can add
to the health and wellness of our ecosystems.
Developing plant-made color encourages us to
think about limits in production and

consumption—limits that are essential to sustaining ecological life. Limits often build creativity.

Gathering rainwater for color alchemy, cooking dinner for friends then making colors from the leftover pits and rinds, enjoying fragrant bouquets and making beautiful hues when they have wilted: developing these plant-made palettes can be a catalyst for wonder, nurturing unique and interconnected spectra of elemental hues and experiences.

4   PERFUME PALETTE

Bitter Orange Peels   Gardenia Seeds   Jasmine Vines

Glowing yellows from bitter orange peels and jasmine vines, the tropical notes of gardenia greens, and the rich, woodsy smells and hues of sandalwood balance this perfect aromatic blend. A perfume-based palette provides an evocative means of deepening your color sense.

Patchouli Leaves   Sandalwood

Bitter Orange Peels

—

Citrus x aurantium

Fragrant bitter orange is a zesty, fresh scent used in foods, perfumes, and cosmetics. Bitter orange peel is one of the most common ingredients used in perfumery—with invigorating and tangy results. It is well known for its balanced bouquet, which blends easily with an array of ingredients. The colors made from bitter orange peels range from bright to light yellows and soft yellow-greens.

1	2
NM	AL
3	4
AL+FE	FE

Gardenia Seeds

—

Gardenia jasminoides

The fragrant white flowers of the gardenia give off one of nature's most intoxicatingly beautiful smells. Originating in Asia, the gardenia plant is an evergreen shrub in the coffee family. Gardenia fruit is prized for its yellow dyes as well as its medicinal properties. The fruit of gardenia is said to "drain fire" within the system of traditional Chinese medicine. Gardenia makes bright yellows and tangy oranges as well as shades of chartreuse.

1 NM	2 AL
3 AL+FE	4 FE

Jasmine Vines

—

Jasminum

Jasmine is prized in many areas of the world for its perfume qualities. It can also be enjoyed as a tea as well as in the garden as an ornamental plant. Jasmine can be used as a subtly beautiful dye, providing light greens, golden yellows, and greenish grays.

1 NM	2 AL
3 AL+FE	4 FE

Patchouli Leaves

Pogostemon cablin

Patchouli has been used for centuries for its strong, woodsy aroma and remains popular today. It is cultivated as an essential oil, an incense, a medicine, an herbal tea, and even an insect repellent. Iconic to the hippie movement in the United States and Europe in the 1960s and '70s, patchouli fell from grace after its cultural heyday but has recently been returning. In the Lamaiacea family of flowering mints, patchouli is a hardy, bushy herb with pale pink and white flowers. The colors made from dried patchouli leaves have a subtle range from beige to brighter yellows, minty greens, and dark teals and deep grays.

1	2
NM	AL
3	4
AL+FE	FE

Sandalwood

Santalum

Sandalwood, with its clean, woodsy, earthy smell,
is highly prized as an essential oil and perfume base
and in aromatherapy. Sandalwood has a long history;
it is used medicinally in Ayurvedic traditions both
as an astringent and an anti-inflammatory, which makes
it great for the skin. The colors made from sandalwood
range from warm, earthy pinks and browns to moody
grays and rich, blueish charcoals.

1 NM	2 AL
3 AL+FE	4 FE

5 FOREST BATHING

Pine Branches   Spruce Cones   Spruce Branches

A walk in the forest can connect you to a soothing palette of greens, grays, and earthy mauves. Awaken the senses with deep, inky blues from spruce boughs, pinks from their cones, golden yellows and earthy golden greens from bracken ferns, and evergreen hues from balsam boughs that are just as fragrant in the dye bath as they are beautiful in tone. Even in the process of gathering, this forest-infused color palette is energizing to the senses and holistically regenerative.

Balsam Fir Branches   Bracken Fern   Birch Bark

Pine Branches

—

Pinus strobus

Pine trees are coniferous evergreens. There are over
126 named species of pine. These trees are long lived and
can survive for more than a thousand years. A tea can
be made from steeping young green pine needles, providing
a good source of vitamins A and C. Pine bark bread can
be made of the inner bark, once ground up as a flour.
These varying shades of pinks to slate grays were created
using the eastern white pine, native to North America
and the official state tree of Maine.

1 NM	2 AL
3 AL+FE	4 FE

Spruce Cones

—

Picea glauca

White spruce is the northernmost tree species of North America. It is very hardy and can live for several hundred years and withstand temperatures well below zero. White spruce seeds disperse at the end of the summer, when their cones dry out and open onto the forest floor. Where spruce cones are common, they can cover the ground in a wonderful seasonal color display. Their smell in the dye bath immediately conjures up a sensory and calming walk in the woods. White spruce cones without a mordant yield blush-pink tones; with iron added, they produce darker purples and greens.

1 NM	2 AL
3 AL+FE	4 FE

Spruce Branches

—

Picea glauca

Spruce is a valuable asset to the boreal and temperate forests of the northern climates, as it holds together the soil. The fresh shoots of spruce are chock-full of vitamin C. The tips of the leaves can make a tasty spruce syrup, and the leaves and branches contain essential oils that can be used to brew spruce beers. Spruce trees are gloriously fragrant; along with pine and balsam, they are often used to accompany winter floral decor and as Christmas trees. If you do not live in a northern climate or are unable to simply prune and harvest from your own backyard, you can reuse seasonal evergreen decorations after the winter holidays. There are thirty-five named species of spruce trees. The boughs, cones, and bark of many types of spruce produce a variety of colors; the ones here were made from the white spruce. All types of spruce tree boughs can make fodder for beautiful hues, typically yellows to cool greens, grays, blues, and even blacks.

1 NM	2 AL
3 AL+FE	4 FE

Balsam Fir Branches

—

Abies balsamea

Balsam is an evergreen tree ranging in size from small
to medium. It thrives in cool climates and loves moisture
at its roots. The tree is a prolific food source for many
northern forest animals, including moose, red squirrels,
and chickadees. The fragrant evergreen boughs are
used decoratively in winter and are a great source
of color throughout the year—even after they have been
enjoyed inside.

1	2
NM	AL
3	4
AL+FE	FE

Bracken Fern

—

Pteridium

Bracken love to grow in marshlands and woodsy thickets; they can also be found at the edge of forests in the Northern Hemisphere. The word *bracken* originates from Old Norse, meaning "fern." Bracken can also become quite invasive, making it a good plant to harvest as a dye or color source, as removing it can aid habitat restoration. Bracken can create hues of warm pink, ochers, and reddish browns.

1 NM	2 AL
3 AL+FE	4 FE

Birch Bark

—

Betula species

The birch is a hardwood tree native to colder northern climates. Birch bark, depending on how it's processed, can produce everything from beautiful, warm golden tones and blush colors to deeper shades of caramel and even dusty pink and mauve. Fortunately, because of the birch's natural preservative properties and its habit of shedding, the bark can be found on the woodland floor, making it easily collected without harm to the tree. (Removing bark directly from live trees can be harmful to their health and growth, so avoid this temptation.) Birch bark is both strong and water resistant, among its many remarkable properties. Since ancient times, birch bark has been used as a building, crafting, and writing material. Birch is also known for its pliability and strength; it can be bent easily and even sewn. The bark of sweet birch can be made into birch beer, which is similar to root beer or sarsaparilla soda.

1	2
NM	AL
3	4
AL+FE	FE

6   SALTWATER COLORS

Seaweed / Bladder Wrack   Iceplant   Dune Sagewort

The alchemy of ocean air and alkaline sandy soil creates coastal color inspiration. Washed-ashore kelp and seaweed can make hues that soothe the senses and bring inspiration from a watery depth. Beachside succulents create soft pinks and deep grays. Coastal sage chaparral makes palettes that thrive in salty soils. Saltwater can even add its own alchemy to the dye bath and be a naturally abundant source of water.

California Sagebrush
Kelp

Seaweed / Bladder Wrack

—

Fucus vesiculosus

Wrack is a seaweed commonly found on the North Atlantic coasts, the North Sea, the Baltic Sea, and the north Pacific Ocean. Revered for its iodine, *Fucus vesiculosus*, or bladder wrack, has been used to treat iodine deficiencies. It is also edible and is easy to obtain through local herbalists or health food stores. Bladder wrack makes warm, sandy hues, from rosy tones to darker, richer browns.

1	2
NM	AL
3	4
AL+FE	FE

Iceplant

—

Carpobrotus edulis

Iceplant is a succulent shrub native to South African coastal regions. Iceplants were first introduced in California to mitigate erosion when railroads were being built along the coastal areas. Because it is a prolific and successful adapter, it competes with many native and rare coastal plants and even alters the soil composition for its future growth. *Carpobrotus* comes from the Greek word *karpos*, which means "edible"; this culinary delicacy can in fact be eaten fresh, pickled, or dried and used in salads. It also makes a gorgeous dye—when used on its own, the plant alone yields pink shades; with alum, peach; and with iron, purple-grays.

1 NM	2 AL
3 AL+FE	4 FE

Dune Sagewort

—

Artemisia pycnocephala

Dune sagewort is native to the West Coast, from Oregon to Central California. A species in the sagebrush family, this plant is highly aromatic and smells just as lovely in a dye bath as it does at the shore. Dune sagewort takes its name from the sandy dunes that protect it. In the dye pot, colors range from golden yellows to deeply rich dark greens.

1 NM	2 AL
3 AL+FE	4 FE

California Sagebrush

—

Artemisia californica

California coastal sage is vital to the coastal chaparral environment. If you live in the right climate—especially where sage grows native—it can be highly beneficial to your garden, both as a drought-tolerant source of lasting beauty and as a readily available, sweet-smelling dye plant. The colors from coastal sage are soothing yellows and greens.

1 NM	2 AL
3 AL+FE	4 FE

Kelp

—

Nereocystis luetkeana

Bull kelp thrives in rough, high-energy coastal waters, largely because of its ability to securely root itself. Bull kelp, which looks like a long whip, often washes to shore when waters are particularly stormy. Most varieties of kelp make rich, soothing tones and can be good sources of inspiration for color choices involving warm, sophisticated neutrals.

1	2
NM	AL
3	4
AL+FE	FE

Landscape Alchemy

Regenerative is a term that is a step beyond *sustainable*. To regenerate is to restore life to a system, to add to it or heal it rather than just to "sustain" the system as it is. Regeneration can frame for us an essential goal by offering evolving ways to renew a system with additional life and energy. This idea can be especially powerful for the design process, as it motivates us to think beyond the boundaries of what we presently think is possible while deeply nourishing the best of what already exists.

Pruning, for example, is one of the primary ways of tending a tree; it provides healthier and more plentiful growth and fruiting. Those pruned branches may then be used further to provide gorgeous natural hues and color combinations.

Cultivating an awareness of plant species that are native to an area, endangered, or both is a good place to begin a regenerative practice. Understanding the relative roles and positions of local plant species in the local ecosystems helps to care for and protect them. When collecting or foraging for ingredients, whether in an urban neighborhood or in the greater wild, it is always important to remember that each of your interactions has an impact.

Likewise, get to know invasive plants that are common where you live. Some plants can be so highly successful that they crowd out other plants, damaging the biodiversity of a region. However, an overabundance of those plants creates an opportunity for experimenting with those color sources that may be helpfully removed from an ecosystem. From day to day and year to year, cultivating ecological care and stewardship by noticing and tending to plants can have a significant effect on their health and balance.

7 CALIFORNIA COASTAL COLORS

Coast Redwood Cones   Horsetail   Wild Fennel

Surfers bobbing in teal and green Pacific waves, cliffs covered in acid yellow from wild fennel flowers, ancient redwoods reaching through the fog—the plant colors made from these California coastal ingredients create a perfect West Coast color palette.

California Poppy   Sticky Monkey Flower   Manzanita Bark

Coast Redwood Cones

—

Sequoia sempervirens

Coast redwoods are the iconic giants of California. Planting these majestic evergreens brings beauty for generations; they can live for over two thousand years and are highly important to forest ecosystems. Redwood cones, collected for their color, are as fragrant in the dye pot as a misty walk in a coastal rain forest and conjure gorgeous pinks, mauves, purples, grays, and blacks.

1 NM	2 AL
3 AL+FE	4 FE

Horsetail

—

Equisetum

As one of the world's most ancient plants, dating to the Paleozoic period over 300 million years ago, horsetail is called by some a living fossil. It grows naturally in California, thriving in coastal creek beds and riverbanks. Horsetail has been used as an herbal remedy for centuries and can be topically applied to the skin to help with wounds and burns. Because of its deep rhizomes and rapid adaptation to new ecosystems, horsetail can often become invasive, making it a resourceful and plentiful raw material for natural colors. Its palette includes soft pinks, golds, grays, and khakis. When applied with other dyes to wool, it can open the material's fiber to accept the other colors more readily.

1 NM	2 AL
3 AL+FE	4 FE

Wild Fennel

—

Foeniculum vulgare

During the summer months in California, hardy and adaptive wild fennel grows prolifically throughout coastal areas. Wild fennel flowers, with their bursts of fluorescent, starlike yellow blooms, drip with pollen at the height of their season—typically from July through September. Once wild fennel is introduced to an area, it can easily take over and outcompete California native plants. With its invasive nature and color-making potential, from fluorescent yellows to dark greens, wild fennel is a bountiful and beautiful natural color source.

1 NM	2 AL
3 AL+FE	4 FE

California Poppy

—

Eschscholzia californica

In the wild every spring, California poppies grow along
the coast, their vibrant orange flowers dotting cliffs
and color coordinating with sunset ocean hues. The silk-
petaled flowers range from yellow to orange, pink, and
red and sometimes are even bicolored. At home in your
own garden, California poppies make beautiful borders and
easily self-seed. They also make an excellent cover crop,
adding nitrogen and other nutrients to the soil. California
poppy petals and leaves make pastel palettes of soft
yellows, greens, teals, and grays.

1 NM	2 AL
3 AL+FE	4 FE

Sticky Monkey Flower

—

Diplacus aurantiacus

Sticky monkey flower grows in the American Southwest and from Oregon through most of California. The Miwok and Pomo people native to coastal California have prized this medicinal plant as a treatment for a variety of ailments, including its topical use to alleviate minor sores and burns. The flowers grow in a variety of colors from reds to whites, most commonly in yellow-orange. Sticky monkey flower grows well in coastal clay soils, even in serpentine-rich ones (which have a unique mineral composition that is inhospitable to some plants). As a native Californian garden plant, sticky monkey flower draws a variety of pollinators, from bees to hummingbirds to butterflies. It's also an important host plant for the common buckeye butterfly (*Junonia coenia*). Orange and yellow sticky monkey flowers produce soft yellows and blue-grays as well as inkier grays, depending on how the color is modified.

1	2
NM	AL
3	4
AL+FE	FE

Manzanita Bark

—

Arctostaphylos

There are over forty species of manzanita in California.
All parts of manzanita can be used to make beautiful colors;
manzanita bark is particularly easy to collect, as it is shed
naturally by the tree. Native Californians created fermented
sodas out of the berries and used the leaves as natural
toothbrushes. Because of the important role it plays
in West Coast biodiversity, manzanita is wonderful to
plant in your yard if you live in that region. The leaves of
manzanitas create beautiful yellows, greens, and grays,
while the bark creates blushing pinks, mauves, deep
purples, grays, and blacks.

1 NM	2 AL
3 AL+FE	4 FE

8   PAINTED DESERT

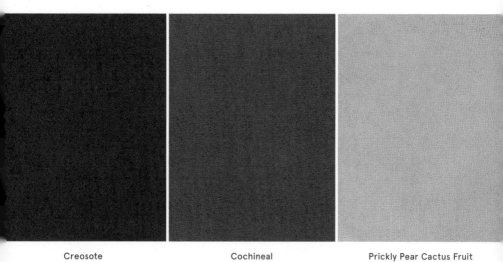

Creosote   Cochineal   Prickly Pear Cactus Fruit

Vibrant color palettes from drought-tolerant desert plants—and insects!—are nothing less than awe inspiring. These beautiful hues from prickly pears, cochineal, purple sage, and creosote glow with beauty reminiscent of a dip-dyed desert sunset.

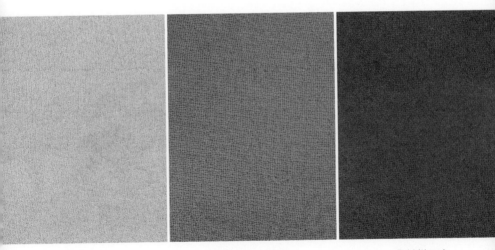

Coyote Bush   Desert Purple Sage   Rabbitbrush

Creosote

—

Larrea tridentata

Larrea tridentata, commonly known as creosote bush, greasewood, or chaparral (when used as a medicinal herb), is an evergreen shrub that grows throughout much of desert California and Baja as well as other parts of the Southwest and Mexico. Its smell is often associated with the scent of rain. Mature chaparral can tolerate the stress of extreme drought. Indigenous peoples of the Southwest believed that chaparral held medicinal qualities, helping with a variety of maladies, from tuberculosis to chicken pox to snakebites. Color from the chaparral plant can range from golden yellows and light oranges to deep greens and grays.

1 NM	2 AL
3 AL+FE	4 FE

Cochineal

—

Dactylopius Coccus x Opuntia

Cochineal is a scale insect whose habitat is cacti in the genus *Opuntia*. Only the females inhabit the nopal cactus, which is native to Mexico, Central and South America, and the Canary Islands and found wild in desert areas of the Southwest, Southern California, and elsewhere in the United States. Cochineal's lightfast deep pinks, reds, and purples have been used since ancient times by the indigenous people of the Americas, including both the Maya and the Aztecs. Today, cochineal is cultivated in Oaxaca, Mexico, and by farmers in Peru, Chile, and the Canary Islands. Cochineal is one of the world's healthiest reds, due to its nontoxic nature. It is often used in food coloring and cosmetics as an alternative to harmful synthetic reds. Because cochineal is pH sensitive, it can provide a wide range of hot pinks, fuchsias, and reds as well as purples, blues, and dark grays, depending on how the color is modified.

1 NM	2 AL
3 AL+FE	4 FE

Prickly Pear Cactus Fruit

—

Opuntia

Prickly pear cacti are native to the Americas; their
beautiful edible fruit is known as *tuna* in Spanish. Enjoyed
both as a food and when made into a drink, prickly pear
fruit must be peeled carefully to avoid the small spines.
Heating the color after fermentation creates warm oranges
and golden tones on wool and silks. When pressed and
used in a cold dye bath, beautiful pink colors can be
produced on wool and silk fibers.

1	2
NM	AL
3	4
AL+FE	FE

Coyote Bush

—

Baccharis pilularis

Coyote bush, also known as chaparral broom,
is naturalized to drought and desert conditions and
common throughout the desert areas of Oregon,
California, and Baja. Coyote bush is a highly adaptable
shrub that's fire resistant when young and green.
The plants spread over a wide territory, causing it to
become invasive. For that reason, it can be readily
available to use as a dye material, depending
on your region. Coyote bush creates bright, bold,
clear yellows as well as vital light greens and deep,
dark gray-greens.

1 NM	2 AL
3 AL+FE	4 FE

Desert Purple Sage

—

Salvia dorrii

Native to the Western deserts of the United States,
Salvia dorrii, also known as desert sage, purple sage,
or tobacco sage, grows throughout the mountainous desert
regions of the western United States, including the Great
Basin region, Death Valley, and into the Mojave Desert.
Desert purple sage is a drought-tolerant woody shrub
in the mint family. Its flowers are very beneficial, attracting
butterflies and hummingbirds while also being deer
and rabbit resistant. Natural dye colors made from desert
purple sage range from bright yellows to deep, rich,
earthy greens.

1 NM	2 AL
3 AL+FE	4 FE

Rabbitbrush

—

Chrysothamnus viscidiflorus

Rabbitbrush, a yellow flowering perennial shrub, can
be brewed as a medicinal tea and has been employed
by many Native American tribes for various purposes.
The Paiute people of Nevada have used yellow rabbitbrush as a remedy for coughs and colds, the Hopi
as a dermatological aid for soothing the skin, and the
Gosiute for the natural latex found in rabbitbrush
as a chewing gum. The Hopi and Navajo also use rabbitbrush as a strong yellow and green dye.

1	2
NM	AL
3	4
AL+FE	FE

9 HĀMĀKUA COAST

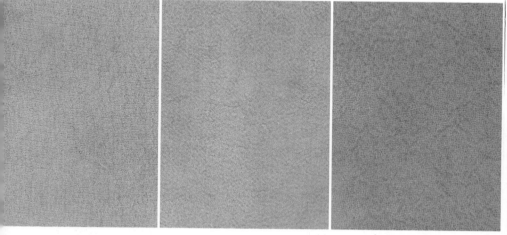

Passionfruit Vines   Sugarcane Husks   Annatto Seeds

This palette, inspired by the agricultural beauty and biodiversity of the Big Island of Hawai'i, includes colors that can be made from plants of the tropical farmlands of the Hāmākua Coast as well as from by-products of the island's local farmers markets. A palette from strawberry guava tree prunings, annatto seeds, coconut husks, red banana peels, and passionfruit vines suggests lush color combinations.

Strawberry Guava Tree Branches   Avocado Rinds   Coconut Husks

Passionfruit Vines

—

Passiflora edulis Sims

Passionfruit, or lilikoi, can grow prolifically in warmer climates, making the leaves, vines, and rinds a plentiful source of dye material. All parts of the passionfruit are edible and when steeped make an excellent tea. Passionfruit vines create a super-fluorescent yellow with an alkaline modifier added as well as deep vibrant greens when iron is added.

1 NM	2 AL
3 AL+FE	4 FE

Sugarcane Husks

—

Saccharum

Sugarcane was originally domesticated in 8000 BCE
in New Guinea. Remnants of Hawai'i's once economically
thriving agricultural sugarcane industry still exist on the
slopes below Mauna Kea on the Big Island, in endless fields
as well as by the side of the road. Sugarcane, a perennial
in the grass family, has long, fibrous stems filled with
sucrose. While the inner stalk provides a sweet treat
for your mouth, its husks and leaves (which were used
to make this palette) create beautiful colors, as does
fermented sugarcane. In Okinawa, Japan, the Ryukyuan
people have cultivated methods of fermentation, called
ugi. Sugarcane can produce different colors depending
on the season when it is harvested. Sugarcane tassels,
which are harvested between June and December, can
create beautiful pinks. The fermented plant can create
yellows and greens in the summer and more neutral
tones in the winter.

1 NM	2 AL
3 AL+FE	4 FE

Annatto Seeds

—

Bixa orellana

Annatto originated in tropical rain forest areas from Mexico to Brazil, where it is prized for its use as a sunscreen and insect repellent, for medicinal purposes, and in ritual as a body paint. Also known as achiote or lipstick tree, annatto is a non-native plant that has become naturalized on the Big Island, where it goes by *alaea laau* or *kumauna*. With its spiky red and orange pods, annatto produces seeds that provide a bright, stable orange dye and a safe, natural food coloring; with iron added it creates beautiful, rich greens.

1	2
NM	AL
3	4
AL+FE	FE

Strawberry Guava Tree Branches

—

Psidium cattleianum

Strawberry guava trees love warm, tropical climates.
Their fruit is often preferred over other types of
guava for its particularly pleasant natural flavor profile.
Strawberry guavas can be peeled or eaten whole;
the seeds are used as a substitute for coffee, and the
leaves are sometimes brewed as a tea. When guava trees
have been domesticated, pruning is essential to shape
them from shrubs into trees and to help them to bear
more fruit. However, despite plentiful economic uses
for the strawberry guava tree, it is considered invasive
in many tropical areas and has become an especially
problematic plant in Hawai'i. As both an invasive species
and an agricultural waste product in the Islands,
it is a raw material ripe for dyeing. Strawberry guava
trees can create peachy pinks to warm oranges, rich
greens, and ochers.

1 NM	2 AL
3 AL+FE	4 FE

Avocado Rinds

—

Persea americana

Common belief is that the first avocado was brought to Hawai'i in the 1800s, when a friend and confidant of Kamehameha the Great, the first king of Hawai'i, brought it on a ship from South America. Today there are hundreds of hybrid varieties of avocados in the islands as a result of cross-pollination. Many of Hawai'i's own avocados were named after the farmers who grew them. Hawai'i produces some of the biggest and best avocados in the world, due especially to its mineral-rich soil and plentiful micro-climates. Avocados in Hawai'i—whether found in generous numbers lying along a jungle path or purchased from the local farmers market—are both tasty and a myriad source of dye material that ranges from pinks into peach and purple-grays into blacks.

1 NM	2 AL
3 AL+FE	4 FE

Coconut Husks

—

Cocos nucifera

Coconuts are among nature's most perfect foods, filled with fiber, vitamins, minerals, and amino acids. The husks of coconuts are incredibly useful as well, their long staple fibers—natural fibers of various lengths that can be twisted into twine, yarn, or rope. Coconut husk can also be burned to ward off mosquitoes. It makes beautiful tropical pinks, ecrus, purples, and dark charcoal grays.

1 NM	2 AL
3 AL+FE	4 FE

10 URBAN FORAGE IS THE NEW BLACK

Acorns   Black Walnut Hulls   Chestnut Husks

Black—that versatile metropolitan muse and go-to shade—can be made naturally from foraged husks, leaves, and hulls collected right off our city sidewalks. This palette highlights the variety and color depth of these new blacks (and charcoals and grays).

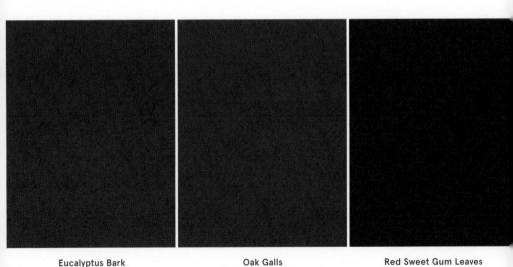

Eucalyptus Bark   Oak Galls   Red Sweet Gum Leaves

Acorns

—

Quercus species

Acorns, stocked with tannins, are a fall foraging staple
known as a protein-filled food source. The variety of
oak determines the tone and color depth of the acorn ink
or dye bath. Acorns yield beautiful colors, from tans
to browns, blues to purples, and deep grays to blacks.

1	2
NM	AL
3	4
AL+FE	FE

Black Walnut Hulls

—

Juglans nigra

Canopies of black walnut trees can often be found in urban centers; they are native to New York City, the epicenter of all-black attire. In the autumn, the nuts can be harvested by the bucketful, even from underproducing trees. Black walnut, more bitter than its English cousin, has been a source of protein in the Americas for thousands of years. Black walnut hulls can be separated from the walnuts, allowing you to enjoy the nut (if it's not too bitter for your taste) as well as the deep, rich colors the green hulls can produce. Remember that if you or someone who will receive the color is allergic to walnuts, the same precautions apply when making or using dyed products as when ingesting the nuts. Black walnuts create stable lightfast and washfast dyes, from deep dark browns when used on their own to solid blacks when iron is added.

1	2
NM	AL
3	4
AL+FE	FE

Chestnut Husks

—

Aesculus hippocastanum

The common horse chestnut is native to southeastern Europe, although it now grows in many northern climates throughout the world. A towering deciduous tree, the chestnut can grow up to seventy-five feet. Chestnut husks can be collected readily throughout late summer to early winter. The husks create beautiful soft pinks, mauves, browns, and dark charcoal grays.

1 NM	2 AL
3 AL+FE	4 FE

Eucalyptus Bark

—

Eucalyptus

Many varieties of eucalyptus trees naturally shed their
bark in large quantities, making foraging easy in urban
environments where these trees are common. Processing
eucalyptus bark is simple and doesn't require heat.
With no mordant, you can get tan and caramel colors,
and with iron added, grays and blacks.

1	2
NM	AL
3	4
AL+FE	FE

Oak Galls

—

Quercus species

Oak galls (also called oak apples) are chock-full of tannins, which can help to bind a wide range of plant-based hues to plant-based fibers; because of this, they are often called "dyer's gold." Oak galls also make an excellent dye on their own. Contrary to what you might think, they are not the fruit of the oak tree but rather the symbiotic product of a wasp that uses the oak as a protective home for its eggs—the oak responds by producing extra tannins, in the process forming the gall. Oak galls can be crushed into a powder for even easier use. They can generate yellows and ochers as well as a range of deep blues, grays, and blacks.

1 NM	2 AL
3 AL+FE	4 FE

Red Sweet Gum Leaves

—

Liquidambar styraciflua

The sweet gum is a deciduous tree common throughout
many urban areas. The leaves turn bright pink and red in
the fall and collect plentiful piles in the streets. A favorite
sensory dye bath, the leaves without a mordant added
make beautiful blush tones and smell like nutmeg.
The colors made from sweet gum leaves range from light
to medium pinks and amber to deep purples, grays,
and blacks.

1	2
NM	AL
3	4
AL+FE	FE

Weeds to Wonder

A weed is defined as a plant that is unwanted.
Tragically, after World War II, weed killers became
popular that contained toxic chemicals, which
are no good for pollinators, people, or our soil
and waterways. At the same time, the production
of toxic synthetic chemicals for fibers and dyes
also ramped up while the disposability of our
materials goods increased. As in so many other
examples, a short-term solution won out over
long-term sustainability.

Yet "weeds" hold valuable medicinal, culinary,
and color-producing properties. They may be
superpowers of the plant world for their ability
to thrive in challenging environments. Weeds such
as oxalis, dandelion, tansy, and nettle all make
wonderful dyes with a range of vibrant hues.

The most tried, true, and safe way of removing weeds is still by pulling or digging them out.
"Weeding your wardrobe" has become the
concept for hands-on parties I've organized to
remove weeds from community gardens,

repurpose them as color producers, and use those colors to add fresh, modern takes to previously discarded or unwanted items. Both the garden and your closet get "weeded," benefitting each. There is a simple, everyday magic in these moments of transformation—the moment when a weed goes from unwanted to wondrous.

Weeds, in fact, hold wonderful promise as sources of color for those willing to do the work. Whether we work in small batches with the weeds found in our own gardens or if in the future large companies research and consider new purposes for invasive species, weeds hold more promise than most appreciate. Valuing and repurposing what we already have may well hold a key to color's evolving role in ecological design processes.

11 IN THE WEEDS

Tansy

Goldenrod

Sourgrass

Weeds are not just wild and unwelcome plants that show up in your garden—they are some of the most powerful plants on the planet. Adaptable to challenging growing environments, they are invariably highly successful at firmly rooting and reproducing. To those who know, weeds have incomparable edible, medicinal, and color-producing qualities.

Queen Anne's Lace   Nettle   Alkanet Root

Tansy

—

Tanacetum vulgar

Tansy is an herbaceous perennial native to temperate regions of Europe and Asia. Since its introduction to other regions, including North America, tansy has become invasive in some areas. Tansy has a long history of medicinal usage dating back at least to the ancient Greeks. Although the flowers and leaves can be quite toxic in large quantities, the plant is still considered curative when used with care. Tansy was grown in the herb gardens of the medieval emperor Charlemagne and by Benedictine monks to treat intestinal issues, rheumatism, fevers, sores, and measles. Tansy was also used as an insect repellent. The colors that can be made from tansy can vary from bright and bold yellows to a range of greens.

1 NM	2 AL
3 AL+FE	4 FE

Goldenrod

—

Solidago

An herbaceous perennial, goldenrod grows bountifully throughout most of North America as well as parts of Mexico, with some species native to South America and Eurasia. Young goldenrod leaves are edible, and the flower can be made into a medicinal tea. In some cultures, goldenrod is considered a symbol of good fortune. It is an excellent pollinator plant, with sweet nectar for bees, wasps, flies, and butterflies. Goldenrod provides brilliantly bright yellows and glowing deep greens.

1	2
NM	AL
3	4
AL+FE	FE

Sourgrass

—

Oxalis pes-caprae

Sourgrass, also known as soursob, soursop, Cape sorrel, English weed, and buttercup oxalis, among other names, is considered an invasive weed. Sourgrass covers much of California in the spring as well as other parts of the world, including its native South Africa and other parts of Africa, Europe, Israel, and Australia. Used as a culinary garnish, sourgrass can also be made into an ointment and used to treat cuts, scrapes, infections, and rashes. The whole plant, including the roots, can be used in the dye bath to make gorgeous, clear florescent yellows, ochers, and deep dark greens. Sourgrass is also pH sensitive; when created with more acidic water it provides very bright yellows and greens and with alkaline water, rusty oranges and deep browns.

1 NM	2 AL
3 AL+FE	4 FE

Queen Anne's Lace

—

Daucus carota

Queen Anne's lace, also known as wild carrot,
is a widespread weed native to temperate Europe
and southwest Asia, though now naturalized in many
other areas of the world, including North America
and Australia. Attracting pollinators such as wasps
to nearby crops, Queen Anne's lace is known
as a beneficial weed. The colors it creates are light
yellows, greens, and grays.

1 NM	2 AL
3 AL+FE	4 FE

Nettle

—

Urtica dioica

Nettles have been used as a food and a medicine since ancient times. Their stalks can be used to make a strong fiber, and they provide a range of natural dye colors, with their tops creating the most vibrant shades in the dye pot. Care should be taken—and gloves worn—when harvesting the plant, as the stinging hairs can be quite painful and difficult to remove from the skin. Nettle creates beautiful color palettes of light greens as well as gray-greens and earthy, rich, deep green-browns.

1	2
NM	AL
3	4
AL+FE	FE

Alkanet Root

—

Alkanna tinctoria

Considered a weed, dyer's alkanet is used on textiles, on wood, as a food coloring, and in wines and other alcoholic beverages. A member of the borage family, alkanet has tiny bright blue flowers in alkaline environments and pink ones in acidic. In folk medicine, alkanet is said to relieve abscesses and inflammation. Alkanet is a perennial in warm zones and a biennial in cold ones. It's known for the silvery blue, red, mauve, purple, and gray colors that can be made from its root.

1 NM	2 AL
3 AL+FE	4 FE

12   YARDAGE

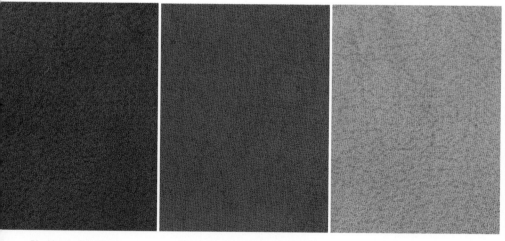

Blackberry Brambles   Dandelion Flowers and Leaves   English Ivy Vines

Many common vines, brambles, and weeds in our own backyards and gardens can provide beautiful dye colors. Before we allow them to become merely green waste, let us appreciate the greens and other hues created from these often overly productive plants.

Morning Glory Vines   Raspberry Brambles   Red Clover

Blackberry Brambles

—

Rubus fruticosus

Many consider blackberries to be a weed because of
their strong root systems and tangled, thorny branches,
which make them tricky in the garden, especially for
children and pets. In the wild, brambles can be difficult
to remove as they constantly spring new shoots. A bramble
is a rough, typically wild, tangled, and prickly shrub,
usually a member of the *rubus* family, which includes
blackberries and raspberries. They can easily overtake
garden spaces, so pruning can be helpful in both domestic
and wild landscapes. Wild blackberries can be one
of late summer's most delicious treats; after pruning,
the brambles themselves make beautiful color ranges,
from pink to green and gray to black.

1 NM	2 AL
3 AL+FE	4 FE

Dandelion Flowers and Leaves

—

Taraxacum officinale

Dandelion is a prolific weed that populates open spaces and gardens with ease. It has been used medicinally for hundreds of years. It's well loved as a nutritious source of greens and made into dandelion tea and wine. Dandelion is best used fresh as a dye—the flowers and leaves can be simmered together for bright, vibrant yellows and greens. Dandelion roots are a bit more difficult to coax but can also be a source of pinks and purples.

1 NM	2 AL
3 AL+FE	4 FE

English Ivy Vines

—

Hedera helix

Ivy includes a group of typically fast-growing, creeping vines, often used in gardens to fill out and cover land-scapes. When the soil is moist and the plant is in shade, it can be aggressively invasive. English ivy can grow to heights of twenty to eighty feet. Colors made from ivy range from light to medium yellows and greenish grays.

1 NM	2 AL
3 AL+FE	4 FE

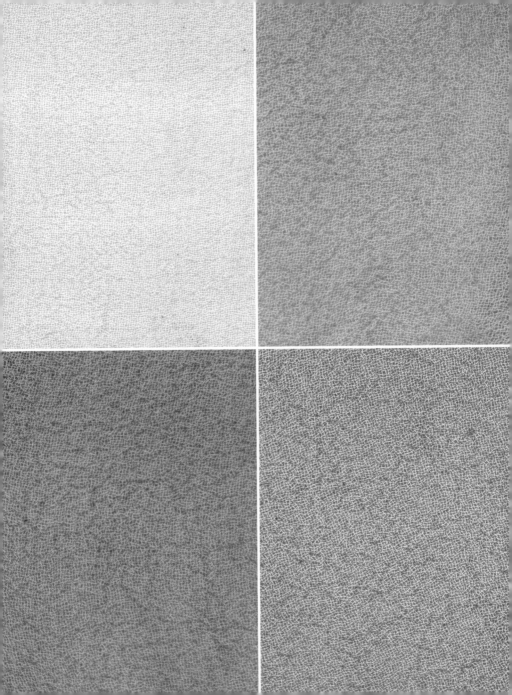

Morning Glory Vines

—

Convollvulaceae

There are almost one thousand varieties of morning glories—the one used here is called "Tie Dye." Morning glories were first cultivated in China for medicinal purposes; the seeds were used as a laxative. Morning glories were later introduced to Japan in the ninth century, and during the Edo period it became very popular as a symbolic and ornamental plant. Japan now leads the world in cultivars of morning glories. Morning glory has become quite invasive in many landscapes, as it climbs and smothers other plants. When you finally cut it back, you'll be rewarded with a wide spectrum of yellows to greens.

1 NM	2 AL
3 AL+FE	4 FE

Raspberry Brambles

—

Rubus fruticosus

Raspberry is a beloved garden planting: the delicious, rich pink berries are popular in jams, jellies, and baking, while the leaves can be brewed as a medicinal herbal tea. Traditionally planted in winter as dormant canes, the plants grow into brambles by the height of the summer season and should be trimmed regularly to avoid spreading. In the wild, raspberries are vigorous and can become invasive in certain areas. Providing plenty of trimmings, raspberry brambles can make colors ranging from bright and rich yellows to tealish greens, grays, and even blacks.

1 NM	2 AL
3 AL+FE	4 FE

Red Clover

—

Trifolium pratense

Native to Europe, Western Asia, and Africa, red clover
has become one of the most common lawn weeds in those
regions. The plant is resourceful, with a deep-reaching
taproot, and can easily become weedy or invasive in many
regions and habitats. Red clover is, however, widely valued
as a cover crop; it adds nitrogen to the soil, which aids
the soil's fertility. There are many medicinal uses for the
red clover plant: it can help with menopause symptoms,
lymphatic issues, and even cancers. The whole red clover
plant can be used to make color from golden yellows
to earthy khaki greens.

1	2
NM	AL
3	4
AL+FE	FE

13 ORCHARD PRUNING

Pear Branches   Cherry Branches   Peach Branches

A palette made by pruning fruit trees provides plentiful options for beautiful hues and at the same time healthier and more productive crops. Pruning fruit trees is best done in late fall through early spring, when the trees are most dormant.

Apple Branches   Plum Branches

Pear Branches

—

Pyrus

There are over three thousand varieties of pears
worldwide. The pear is native to the region of Western
Europe through North Africa. Evidence that pears have
been eaten since prehistoric times has been found
near modern-day Lake Zürich. The Romans were the
first known to have cultivated the pear; their cookbooks
recommend stewing them and even making soufflés.
Pruning pear trees, like most fruit-bearing trees,
is best done in the winter when the tree is dormant.
Its cuttings yield pink, salmon, brown, and mauve.

1 NM	2 AL
3 AL+FE	4 FE

Cherry Branches

—

Prunus avium

There are over four hundred species in the *Prunus*
family, also known as the stone fruit family, which includes
plums and peaches in addition to cherries. The species
of *Prunus* are well spread throughout the world in its
temperate regions. Wild cherry trees can often be found
in parks and growing along the edges of woodlands.
Domesticated cherry trees benefit from being pruned
in dormant times of the year, when the tree is not actively
fruiting. Cherry branches can produce gorgeous hues
of lilacs, peachy plums, and deep mauves.

1 NM	2 AL
3 AL+FE	4 FE

Peach Branches

—

Prunus persica

The peach tree originated in the area now Iran. The ancient Chinese believed that the peach tree held more vitality than any other tree, as its blossoms came out so readily before the leaves. Peach branches were also used to ward off evil energy and influences. The pruned branches of the peach tree can create lush, soft pinks, mauves, and purple-gray.

1 NM	2 AL
3 AL+FE	4 FE

Apple Branches

—

Malus pumila

The apple tree originated in central Asia, where its original relatives can still be found. With its prolific religious and mythological associations, it is one of the oldest, if not the oldest, trees to be cultivated. Today more than 7,500 cultivars of apples are known. Apple branches and barks can create a palette from peach to yellows, greens, and rich dark browns.

1 NM	2 AL
3 AL+FE	4 FE

Plum Branches

—

Prunus domestica

The remains of plums from neolithic times have been found in archaeological dig sites. Plum trees have an incredible pollination rate, as most of the tree is covered in blossoms in the spring. Plums are delicious when eaten fresh as well as in jams and jellies and even when made into wine. Its shades are warm pinks, dark green-grays, and blacks.

1 NM	2 AL
3 AL+FE	4 FE

Cultivating Color

Gardening for color and making color can
become a form of symbiotic storytelling, a con-
versation between two practices that cultivate
ecological care and offer unparalleled inspiration
for witnessing beauty, whether in the harvest
of an heirloom rainbow carrot or the variety of
hues its tops can create.

While I love to make colors from foraged
wayside weeds or forgotten compost, every plant
ultimately comes from a seed. Having grown
up on a farm, I quickly recognized when I began
my teaching career how wondrous it was for my
students to experience how a seed can grow
into a powerful source for food, medicine, and
natural color before being composted into its
underlying nutrients for reuse by future generations. Over the years, saving seeds from my
color-producing plants has become a profound
way for me to support healthier-hued cycles.

Growing your own color from edible plants,
medicinal plants, heirloom dye plants, or

even plants selected especially for beneficial ecologies can provide beautiful palettes tuned to every season and occasion. Natural colors can be even more vital when they are linked to healthy gardening and farming systems and the cascade of positive benefits that extend from them. Organic gardening in your own backyard or in your local community ensures food safety and food security and at the same time supports beneficial insects and pollinators, like bees, butterflies, and hummingbirds—and also feeds us with its own natural beauty.

14 POLLINATOR PALETTE

Coreopsis Flowers   Red Poppy Flowers   Hopi Black Dye Sunflower Seeds

242

Some of the most beautiful flowers and foliage in the garden are also the best for plant pollinators. But after these vibrant blooms are enjoyed in their natural environment by beneficial birds, bees, butterflies, and moths and their petals start to peak, they can still provide awe-inspiring color palettes with a warm natural glow for many years afterward. From dyer's coreopsis to red poppies, Hopi black dye sunflowers, and black scabiosa, the world abounds in plants that can make beautiful colors and also bring beneficial wildlife into the garden. A pollinator palette can captivate the senses and sweeten the process of renewing our landscapes at the very same time.

Pincushion Flowers   Echinacea   Yellow Cosmos Flowers

Coreopsis Flowers

—

Coreopsis tinctoria

Native to North America, coreopsis depends on bees
for pollination and is a common wildflower in the United
States, especially throughout the plains. Beekeepers
consider all types of coreopsis to be great sources of
pollen and nectar for honey making. Its gorgeous dark
brown and red centers in combination with its sunny
yellow petals make these flowers striking in both the
garden and in cut-flower bouquets. Coreopsis produces
among the most beautiful, vital yellows and oranges
as well as dark greens with iron added.

1 NM	2 AL
3 AL+FE	4 FE

Red Poppy Flowers

—

Papaver rhoeas

One of the most prolific wildflowers in the world, the
red poppy is native to most of Eurasia, North Africa,
and Central Europe. Its timeless beauty radiates from its
wavering papery petals. Red poppy is an excellent home
remedy for sore throats and can be used as a homeopathic
sleep aid. These flowers make beautiful, saturated colors
when extracted in a dye bath, from blues to fuchsia
and purples and dark blues to grays, depending on pH.

1 NM	2 AL
3 AL+FE	4 FE

Hopi Black Dye Sunflower Seeds

—

Helianthus annuus

A traditional heirloom dye source used by the Hopi
for both their wool and basketry, the sunflower was one
of the first domesticated plants. Archaeologists have
found evidence of its use by human groups dating back
to the Middle Archaic period. The seeds are easy to
save and edible, and they impart valuable nutritional oils.
The Hopi black sunflower is an excellent pollinator plant
and provides beautiful annual dye color from year to
year. The flowers of Hopi sunflowers yield bright yellow,
and the seeds provide heirloom-quality, lightfast purple,
blue, and black, depending on the modifier.

1 NM	2 AL
3 AL+FE	4 FE

Pincushion Flowers

—

Scabiosa atropurpurea

Black and purple scabiosa, with their deep-colored
flowers and delicious nectar, are some of the best flowers
for drawing bees and birds to the garden. Also known
as the pincushion flower, it self-seeds from year to year.
Its inspiring form can add depth to the landscape and life
to a cut-flower bouquet. Black and purple scabiosa make
an amazing range of natural colors in the dye pot, which
shift and change easily depending on the pH of water
or an added modifier. The color ranges from purples and
pinks to teals, greens, and inky dark blues.

1 NM	2 AL
3 AL+FE	4 FE

Echinacea

—

Echinacea purpurea

Echinacea flowers are a gorgeous addition to the garden and wonderful for pollinators. The flower is a powerful herbal remedy that boosts the immune system and can also be used to reduce skin inflammation and acne. Echinacea can create effervescent yellows, light and minty greens, and earthy, cool dark green tones.

1 NM	2 AL
3 AL+FE	4 FE

Yellow Cosmos Flowers

—

Cosmos sulphureus

The bright, sunny flowers of yellow cosmos, also known as sulphur cosmos, have been used to make a yellow-orange dye in South America since ancient times. These flowers are hardy annuals and thrive in alkaline soil. All cosmos attract birds and butterflies, including monarchs. The colors range from yellows to orange and light to dark greens.

1 NM	2 AL
3 AL+FE	4 FE

15 DYE GARDEN

Fermented Japanese
Indigo Leaves

Fresh-Leaf Japanese Indigo

Madder Root

Indigo, madder root, weld, and dyer's chamomile,
four of the most ancient, primary plant-based dyes,
can be dye-garden staples for your own grown-from-
seed rainbow. Japanese indigo produces deep organic
blues and—if you have freshly harvested leaves—
an effervescent turquoise. Madder root yields pinks,
corals, and deep, deep earthy reds. Weld, reaching
toward the sun with yellow blooms, makes brilliant
shades while attracting bees happy to collect its
pollen. Dyer's chamomile is both easy to grow and
drought tolerant; its feathery leaves and bright orange
and yellow flowers contribute aromatherapy to your
flower beds and saturated yellows and greens to
a garden-grown color wheel.

Weld   Dyer's Chamomile

Fermented Japanese Indigo Leaves

—

Persicaria tinctoria

A flowering plant in the buckwheat family, Japanese indigo is native to Eastern Europe and Asia. Easy to grow in temperate climates, the plant has the ability to self-seed. Otherwise, saving and using the fresh seed from year to year is the best way to replant. In Japan, the word *kachi* was used to describe the color, and as it also translates as "win," it may be the reason why samurai particularly loved indigo for its good luck. Indigo is a natural insecticide, and its antiseptic properties make it popular as a color for work wear worldwide. The darker the indigo cloth, the more beneficial to the wearer for its topical medicinal use.

1 DIP	2 DIPS
3 DIPS	4 DIPS

Fresh-Leaf Japanese Indigo

—

Persicaria tinctoria

One of the best reasons to grow Japanese indigo from seed in your own dye garden is that you will have plenty of fresh indigo leaves to work with. The leaves, when crushed into a poultice, create stunning turquoise colors with the addition only of enough cold water to cover the materials you wish to dye.

1 DIP	2 DIPS
3 DIPS	4 DIPS

Madder Root

—

Rubia tinctorum

Madder root, used as a colorant since ancient times,
is a miraculous and medicinal source of red dye. Early use
of the plant has been traced as far back as 5500 BCE
in Abydos, Egypt, where it was used as a colorant to dye
flax threads bright red, and 3000 BCE, in Mohenjo Daro
in modern-day Pakistan. Much later, in France, it was used
to craft both a red dye and an alcoholic spirit. Madder
root, the most primary botanically based red color source,
can take up to seven years before a significant harvest
occurs. The long wait for this ultimate slow-grown natural
color is well worth it. Madder dyes do not require
a mordant and are lightfast and washfast on all types
of fabrics. Madder root makes colors from light pinks
to coral, dark orange, and rich dark reds.

1 NM	2 AL
3 AL+FE	4 FE

Weld

—

Reseda luteola

Weld, also known as dyer's rocket, dyer's weld, or dyer's weed, is native to Eurasia and can be found in North America as an introduced species or a common weed. Weld was used intensively as a dye in Medieval Europe, particularly in France, which exported it as a major crop for some time. The widespread commercial use of weld as a dye came to an end in the early twentieth century, when synthetic dyes came into fashion. Weld makes colors from bright, washfast yellows to solid light and dark greens.

1	2
NM	AL
3	4
AL+FE	FE

Dyer's Chamomile

—

Anthemis tinctoria or *Cota tinctoria*

Dyer's chamomile, sometimes called Golden Marguerite, is a member of the sunflower family that is native to Europe, the Mediterranean, and Western Asia. These high-yield, low-maintenance flowers produce a very stable yellow dye that is well suited for overdyeing with indigo for true bright greens; for pairing with madder root for rich, stable corals and oranges; or for providing a warm yellow to contrast with weld's cool yellows. Blooming mid- to late summer, dyer's chamomile attracts bees, butterflies, and other pollinating insects to the garden. It is known medicinally to be a good topical remedy for insect bites and a soothing poultice for aching muscles. Harvesting the flowers before they begin to wilt will encourage your plants to keep producing. The silvery blue-green, feathery leaves and bright gold-orange and yellow flowers have a distinct aromatic herbal essence, similar to tansy or yarrow—contributing a wonderful sensory experience to your garden.

1	2
NM	AL
3	4
AL+FE	FE

16   ZEN GARDEN

Black Bamboo Leaves   Jade Plant Leaves   Camellia Flowers

Since the fourteenth century, Zen Buddhists have created meditation gardens with carefully arranged intentionally austere elements. Tending to a garden is much like curating a contemplative color palette. This palette reuses by-products of plants that can often be found as companions in Zen gardens—from black bamboo prunings to fallen camellia flowers and loquat and Japanese maple leaves.

Red Japanese Maple Leaves   Loquat Leaves

Black Bamboo Leaves

—

Phyllostachys nigra

One of the most striking bamboo varieties because of its beautiful coloring, black bamboo is well loved as a basketry and building material. Bamboo shoots are edible; planting bamboo helps to stabilize soil and control erosion. In the garden, black bamboo can grow up to fifty feet tall, providing visual privacy and acting as a lovely sound barrier that can foster a sense of peace and tranquility. Its leaves and branches create a calming color palette with shades of light yellows and greens.

1	2
NM	AL
3	4
AL+FE	FE

Jade Plant Leaves

—

Crassula ovata

The jade plant is a favorite choice to train into a bonsai tree, as it is easy to care for, prune, and shape. Also known as the lucky plant or money tree, jade, a popular succulent, is easy to propagate in the garden by just snipping off a few larger branches. Jade leaves and stems make surprising color palettes, spanning from light pinks and lavenders to deep blues, purples, and blacks.

1 NM	2 AL
3 AL+FE	4 FE

Camellia Flowers

—

Camellia japonica

Camellias were cultivated in Chinese and Japanese gardens for centuries before they were first seen in Europe. Today there are over three thousand cultivars and hybrids of this evergreen shrub. *Camellia japonica* is one of the species known to be more than five hundred years old. Camellia flowers create delicate shades of pink, lavender, blue-gray, and purple.

1 NM	2 AL
3 AL+FE	4 FE

Red Japanese Maple Leaves

—

Acer palmatum

Japanese maples are a focal point of beauty in the garden. Their sculptural elegance and intricate leaves inspire awe. One of the most versatile garden plants, with over one thousand cultivars, Japanese maples are graceful deciduous trees. Depending on the cultivar, the leaves turn bright red in the fall. They can be collected from the ground and produce beautiful palettes from cool light pinks to blues, purples, grays, and blacks.

1 NM	2 AL
3 AL+FE	4 FE

Loquat Leaves

—

Eriobotrya japonica

The loquat tree is known for its ornamental beauty and its sweet and nutritious fruit as well as the medicinal teas that can be made from its leaves. This tree originated in China but was brought to Japan, where it has been cultivated for more than one thousand years. Over this time it has become naturalized in many other areas of the world. *Biwa cha* is an herbal tea made from loquat leaves in Japan. The leaves are a traditional cure for itchy skin, eczema, bronchitis, and coughs, and they are also anti-inflammatory. The leaves and branches yield a beautiful dye of glowing pinks, peach, coral, and soft, warm red; with iron added, the colors can shift to purple, gray, dark blue, or black.

1 NM	2 AL
3 AL+FE	4 FE

17　HEIRLOOM HUES

Hopi Red Dye Amaranth   Globe Artichoke Leaves   Blue Corn Cobs

These heirloom fruits and vegetables are all harvested in late summer and early fall. Their stunning seasonal colors are the collective result of the individuals, communities, and cultures that have saved them and cultivated them to benefit generations yet to come. These important heirloom varietals continue to exist only because of those who have come before, who have chosen to be the keepers of their biodiversity—of their beauty, color, and flavor—for hundreds, even thousands of years.

Mission Black Fig Leaves   Green Persimmon Fruit

Hopi Red Dye Amaranth

—

Amaranthus cruentus x *A. powellii*

Originally grown as a dye by the southwestern Hopi Nation, this grain has the reddest seeds of any amaranth variety known. It is high in protein and can be readily saved, as the plant provides a plentiful harvest. Amaranth can grow to four to six feet and is a gorgeous addition to any fall garden. As a dye, Hopi red dye amaranth prefers cold- and low-temperature processing to achieve warm tones, where the colors can range from pale to bright pinks and fuchsia.

1 NM	2 AL
3 AL+FE	4 FE

Globe Artichoke Leaves

—

Cynara scolymus

Globe artichoke is an open-pollinated variety of artichoke from Italy and elsewhere in the Mediterranean region. These tender, purple artichoke heads are cold and heat resistant. The leaves and stems of the artichoke plant can offer generous amounts of raw food waste to use in the dye pot after dinner has finished. Artichokes range from tawny yellows to deeper khakis and greens.

1	2
NM	AL
3	4
AL+FE	FE

Blue Corn Cobs

—

Zea mays L.

Blue corn, whose heirloom varieties include Hopi blue
and Yoeme blue, was traditionally cultivated by the Hopi,
Pueblo, and other southwestern people. Blue corn meal,
chips, and tortillas have become a food-industry favorite
in recent years, boosting the cobs' availability as a compost
color source. Because of their high level of the flavonoid
anthocyanin, blue corn cobs produce colors that are quite
sensitive to pH shifts. They can create palettes of pink and
purple with acidic soil, water, or additives or more blue,
gray, green, or black with alkaline additives.

1	2
NM	AL
3	4
AL+FE	FE

HEIRLOOM HUES

Black Mission Fig Leaves

—

Ficus carica

The delicious and popular black mission fig has been
native to the United States since 1768, when Franciscan
missionaries introduced the variety in San Diego, California.
With its dark purple outer skin and sweet, pink, fleshy
fruit, the mission fig later became the main fig crop
planted throughout California. Planting a mission fig brings
sweet and succulent fruit to your own backyard, and
the fallen deciduous leaves in late summer and early fall
provide lovely hues of light yellows and bountiful greens.

1 NM	2 AL
3 AL+FE	4 FE

Green Persimmon Fruit

—

Diospyros kaki

In Japan there are no less than one thousand varieties of persimmon. Despite this dizzying abundance, they break down into two basic types: sweet and astringent. While sweet persimmons are consumed for their flavor, it is the fermented juice of the unripe astringent persimmon that is used to make *kakishibu*, meaning "astringent persimmon," which has been used in Japan as a dye and folk medicine since at least the eighth century. Prized for its antibacterial qualities, it was applied to skin for burns and used to lower blood pressure and even to cure a hangover. The tannins in persimmon leaves were also used to protect sushi from spoiling. *Kakishibu* requires no heat or additional mordants, creating colors from warm peach, oranges, and gray-purples to dark grays.

1 NM	2 AL
3 AL+FE	4 FE

Compost Colors

Although both food and natural fiber and dyes used in clothing and textiles are so biodegradable that they often have left no traces as artifacts, the two have been linked in practical and creative collaborations throughout human history, as creating natural color was once fully in sync with cooking and the making of medicine. Many natural dye ingredients are also medicinal or the by-products of edible plants.

Honoring plants for their multiple purposes can help us to redirect what could otherwise become waste, transforming leftover raw materials into something beautiful, stylish, and meaningful. Everyday waste products from our kitchens, restaurants, and grocery stores—such as onion skins and pomegranate rinds—can be upcycled to extend and expand their value into the realm of color. Making natural color from the by-products of fruits and vegetables can be a very powerful sensory and creative act—much like knowing where your food comes from, or, better yet, learning to grow food and cook it yourself.

What we consider valuable is always changing. Carrot tops can provide gorgeous gold and green colors. At one point, they were grown specifically for the tops rather than the root, as they are very medicinal and flavorful, yet today we tend to just toss them out (if they have not already been removed by the grocer).

Waste from our food supply is one of the single largest problems in US municipal waste. By understanding the plants we eat, we learn how to reduce that waste and use resources more wisely in our homes and communities. At the same time, more opportunities arise for versatility in our uses for those plants—whether they be culinary, medicinal, cultural, or ecological. Working with plant color can be an easy and accessible way of becoming in sync with the cycles of our ecologies and applying that knowledge directly to art and design practices. Natural color created by the seeds, tops, and peels of local fruits and vegetables can connect us to healthier places, restore our own health, and renew our purpose.

18   COMPOST COLORS

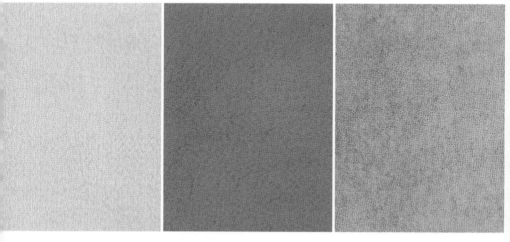

Avocado Pits   Golden Onion Skins   Carrot Tops

Natural color can be abundantly hidden within everyday produce, as the by-products of common fruits and vegetables hold a rainbow array of hues. Compost colors can be made from discarded carrot tops, citrus peels, and pomegranate rinds. Have your color and eat it, too!

Pomegranate Rinds   Mandarin Peels   Black Bean Water

Avocado Pits

—

Persea americana

The avocado tree is thought to have originated in south-central Mexico. The oldest pit ever found dates back ten thousand years. In recent years, the popularity of its fruit, rich in healthy fats, has only grown, making avocado pits and rinds ever more prevalent for use as a dye source before they hit the compost pile. Avocado pits can make beautiful pinks and even dark mauves and reds without the additional use of a mordant. Adding iron can shift these colors to purples, grays, dark blues, and blacks.

1	2
NM	AL
3	4
AL+FE	FE

Golden Onion Skins

Allium cepa

The humble golden onion and its papery skin, so easily overlooked, make some of the best colors. Onions are cultivated and used around the world. They are easy to store and add medicinal qualities and flavor to the cooking process. Onion skins are readily available in large quantities for bigger projects if you make friends with your local produce sellers. From bright and golden yellows to deep, rusty reds and oranges, onion skins create beautiful, lasting colors. With iron added, color from golden onion skins can shift from yellows and oranges to greens, ochers, and deep brown.

1 NM	2 AL
3 AL+FE	4 FE

Carrot Tops

—

Daucus carota

Carrots were once grown for their tops as well as their
roots and were used as a highly medicinal food source.
In carrot tops we see a prime example of how much we've
forgotten and how many plant uses have fallen out of favor.
Carrot tops are an excellent dye source; the colors range
from bright yellows to light greens and dark green to grays.

1 NM	2 AL
3 AL+FE	4 FE

Pomegranate Rinds

—

Punica granatum

The pomegranate originated in Iran and northern India and has been cultivated around the world. Pomegranates, known and loved for their nutritious, fuchsia-colored antioxidant seeds and juice, are now widely used in garnishes, smoothies, and alcoholic beverages, making the rinds excellent candidates for compost color. Pomegranate rinds, rich in tannins, are not only among the most stable dyes for all types of natural fibers but also act as a wonderful mordant to help other dyes become more stable on cottons, linens, hemps, and other plant-based materials.

1	2
NM	AL
3	4
AL+FE	FE

Mandarin Peels

—

Citrus reticulata

Citrus peels can create glowing yellow colors as well as a diversity of light greens and grays. Mandarin peels, due to their darker, concentrated colors, make particularly beautiful hues. Mandarin fruit is the most frequently cultivated citrus fruit in China, tropical Asia, Korea, the Mediterranean, and Florida. Mandarins ripen between November and December, providing an excellent source of vitamin C in the winter. Mandarins, tangerines, and satsumas are considered gifts of good fortune and auspiciousness for Lunar New Year. Citrus peels are particularly slow to break down in compost, so the soaking involved in using them as dye material helps them to compost more efficiently. As pesticides can accumulate in the peels of fruits, organic citrus provides the healthiest natural color. Mandarin peels make pretty, radiant yellows and zesty light yellow-greens.

1 NM	2 AL
3 AL+FE	4 FE

Black Bean Water

—

Phaseolus vulgaris

Soaking dried black beans overnight is a win-win for
the cooking and dye pots, as you can eat your beans
and reuse the soaked water to make a beautiful range
of colors, from pinks to purples, dark blues, and grays—
even greens and turquoise. Colors from black beans
are pH sensitive—in general, the more acidic the water,
the warmer the tone, with more alkaline water bringing
out the blues and the greens.

1	2
NM	AL
3	4
AL+FE	FE

19   TO A TEA

Earl Grey Tea   Matcha Green Tea   Yerba Maté

Making dyes can be just as easy as brewing your favorite tea—literally. This palette shows the range of beautiful tones that can be made, given the nuances of some of the world's most-loved tea varieties. Saving your tea bags—from Earl Grey to matcha, rooibos, and yerba maté—is a wonderful way to reduce waste and brew beautiful hues. Teas, which often have naturally occurring tannins, can provide mordants for other colors, especially on plant-based fibers. The astringent properties of many teas also can help to disinfect and purify fibers or cloth.

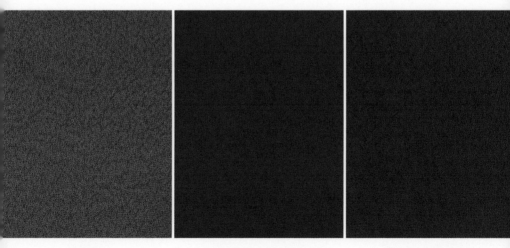

Rooibos · Gunpowder Green Tea · Himalayan White Tea

Earl Grey Tea

—

Camellia sinensis + Citrus bergamia

Earl Grey is an aromatic black tea flavored with
bergamot oil, which is made from the essence of the
sour orange peel. Bergamot is a subspecies of the bitter
orange grown predominately in Italy and France. It was
added to black tea in Europe during the 1800s as a way
to imitate more expensive and aromatic Chinese teas.
In addition to being a popular tea, Earl Grey is often
used to flavor cakes, chocolate, and ice cream as well
as other sweet delicacies and sauces. High in tannins,
black tea can act as a mordant to prepare fibers to take
other natural dyes or to make beautiful neutrals from
ecru to warmer tans, grays, and blacks.

1	2
NM	AL
3	4
AL+FE	FE

Matcha Green Tea

—

Camellia sinensis

Green tea is wonderful for the skin and highly astringent, making it a great choice as a medicinal dye. Matcha is a powdered green tea known for its strong antioxidant properties. Its origins trace back thousands of years in Japan. Samurai were said to drink it to increase energy in battle, and as monks did to increase alertness while maintaining a meditative flow. Matcha is still used in a variety of specialty foods and drinks for its health benefits, beautiful natural food coloring, and flavor. According to the experts, the greener the matcha, the more beneficial its properties.

1 NM	2 AL
3 AL+FE	4 FE

Yerba Maté

—

Ilex paraguariensis

Yerba maté is used to make the beverage maté,
a well-loved drink, especially in northern Argentina,
Uruguay, Paraguay, and southern Brazil. Yerba maté
is now more widely available and enjoyed throughout
the world. Its origin is traced back to consumption
by the indigenous Guaraní and Tupí people of South
America. The leftovers from brewing yerba maté make
yellowy, bright, and dark greens.

1 NM	2 AL
3 AL+FE	4 FE

Rooibos

—

Aspalathus linearis

Also known as red bush, rooibos is a broom-like
member of the Fabacae family. It has been popular
as a tea in South Africa for centuries and is now common
in many other areas of the world as well. Rooibos grows
only in a small microclimate of the Western Cape province
of South Africa. The plant has a symbiotic relationship
with that ecosystem; concerns persist about the impact
of climate change on the plant's future survival. The tea
is prepared with both leaves and stems. The higher the
leaf content, the darker the grade of tea and the darker
the color, whether pink, ocher, or deep gray-green.

1 NM	2 AL
3 AL+FE	4 FE

Gunpowder Green Tea

—

Camellia sinensis

Gunpowder green tea, also called pearl tea or bead tea, is a type of Chinese tea made from leaves that have been rolled into individual balls. The origin of its name in English, gunpowder green, may be connected to the likeness of these rolled leaves to shot; when heat is added, the leaf quickly unfurls, like a tiny explosion. The tea often carries a rich, smoky flavor. The colors made from gunpowder green tea range from tans to peachy pinks, oranges, mauve, dark gray-purples, and blacks.

1	2
NM	AL
3	4
AL+FE	FE

Himalayan White Tea

Camellia sinensis

Himalayan white tea is made from the younger or minimally processed leaves of *Camellia sinensis*. Processing determines the difference between white, green, and black tea as well as each tea's specific flavor and other qualities (all three colors of tea are made from *Camellia sinensis*). The palette of Himalayan white tea ranges from gold to oranges, grays, and blacks.

1 NM	2 AL
3 AL+FE	4 FE

20 TROPICAL PUNCH

Rambutan Peels   Mangosteen Rinds   Purple Passionfruit Rinds

Luscious colors can be created from the by-products of edible and drinkable tropical fruits and flowers. Mango peels can yield dark purple-grays, bright peach from mangosteen peels, dark blacks from rambutan skins, lilac from purple passionfruit peels, and bright pink from hibiscus flowers. All add an extra tropical punch to this gorgeous, tropically made compost color palette.

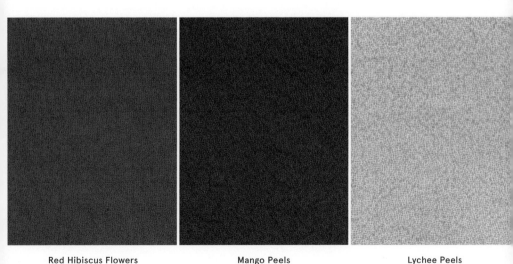

Red Hibiscus Flowers   Mango Peels   Lychee Peels

Rambutan Peels

Nephelium lappaceum

Known for their unusual, hairlike red and green spikes, rambutan fruit are sweet and tangy, with a hint of sour. Thailand is the largest producer of rambutans. The outer skin contains flavonoids with a variety of healthy properties. Packed with concentrated tannins, rambutan peels hold great potential as a by-product of the tropical fruit industry. Colors created can vary from tans to rich yellows and golds to blues and blacks.

1 NM	2 AL
3 AL+FE	4 FE

Mangosteen Rinds

—

Garcinia mangostana

Mangosteen is an evergreen tropical tree originating in the Malay Archipelago and the Moluccas of Indonesia. It has been grown in Malaysia, Borneo, the Philippines, and other parts of Southeast Asia as well as Sumatra since ancient times. The fruit is now cultivated in Southeast Asia, Southern India, South America, Hawai'i, California, Florida, and the Caribbean. Mangosteen fruit is tangy, fleshy, and sweet. The purple rinds of the mangosteen are inedible but can be used to create a range of hues, from pinks and light oranges to dark blues and blacks.

1 NM	2 AL
3 AL+FE	4 FE

Purple Passionfruit Rinds

—

Passiflora edulis Sims

Grown in tropical and subtropical areas, this perennial vine produces a sweet, seedy fruit, eaten on its own or as a juice. Dark purple passionfruit is less acidic and is often considered slightly tastier than the yellow fruit variety. Purple passionfruit rinds make a beautiful range of colors, from pinks and lilacs to teal-grays and dark grays.

1 NM	2 AL
3 AL+FE	4 FE

Red Hibiscus Flowers

—

Hibiscus sabdariffa

Hibiscus is enjoyed as a tea and a drink in many regions throughout the world. Red hibiscus flowers are loved for their bright, bold color and for their tart flavor as well for their health benefits, as they contain lots of vitamin C. They therefore hold great potential for reuse as by-products of the juice and tea industries. The *Hibiscus* genus contains several hundred species, which are native to temperate, subtropical, tropical, and warm climates around the world. Hibiscus hues made from deep-colored petals can range from light pink and magenta to purple, dark blues, blacks, and even greens, depending on pH shifts.

1 NM	2 AL
3 AL+FE	4 FE

Mango Peels

Mangifera indica

A tropical stone fruit, the ripe and juicy mango is a tasty treat and makes delicious juice. The majority of its species are found in tropical nature as wild mangoes. The genus belongs to the cashew family, and the trees are native to South Asia. Mangoes have been cultivated throughout most tropical regions of the world and are distributed worldwide. Mango peels are a major by-product of the tropical fruit industry. Natural colors created from the peels can range in hue from light yellows to darker golds, and, with iron added, yield stunning rich purples and dark grays and blacks.

1 NM	2 AL
3 AL+FE	4 FE

Lychee Peels

—

Sapindaceae

Coming from a tall evergreen tree native to China, the lychee fruit is small and fleshy with pink to red peels that are inedible but very easy to remove. The fruit has a floral smell and an especially perfumed, sweet taste. Lychees are stocked with vitamin C. Lychee peels make excellent colors, from pinks to peach and deep blues, purples, and even natural blacks.

1	2
NM	AL
3	4
AL+FE	FE

21   MELLOW YELLOWS

Chardonnay Grapevines   Hops   Indica Stems

These mellow yellows are by-products of hops left over from brewing beer, stems and leaves from the hemp and cannabis industries, juniper berries from making gin, vineyard prunings for wine, and *artemisia absinthium*, the key plant-based ingredient in the infamous absinthe cocktail.

Juniper Berries   Absinthe

Chardonnay Grapevines

—

Vitis vinifera

Chardonnay is a green grape used to produce full-bodied white wine. The variety originated in the Burgundy region of France and has become the most planted wine grape in the United States. Pruning vineyards and working with fallen grapes provide prime opportunities to locate your practice within a color terroir. Light yellows and warm golden tones abound, along with rich dark greens.

1 NM	2 AL
3 AL+FE	4 FE

Hops

—

Humulus lupulus

Hops are a bitter aromatic agent used to flavor, preserve, and stabilize beer as well as to provide flavor for other drinks, including herbal teas and sodas. It's the resin of the hops flower that is responsible for the bitterness. Hops can also be used medicinally as an herbal remedy for sleeplessness, anxiety, restlessness, and insomnia. With the rise of the craft beer and home-brewing movements, leftover, reusable hops and other by-products of the beer-making process are becoming ever more accessible as dye ingredients. Cultivating hops in one's own garden can also be deeply rewarding. Hops are climbing, weedy vines that can grow to twenty-five feet or more in height, giving them plentiful leaves and vines—and making the excess and prolific green waste of the plant a wonderful candidate for the dye pot. Hues made from both the vines and flowers can range from rich, bright yellows and golds to deep dark greens.

1 NM	2 AL
3 AL+FE	4 FE

Indica Stems

—

Cannabis indica

Cannibis indica is a strain of the small *Cannabaceae*
family of flowering plants, which includes hemp, hops,
and marijuana. With the legalization of marijuana in
several US states and Canada, common by-products
of the cannabis industry offer new options in the realm
of dyes and fiber. Indica, which is a quick-growing strain
of cannabis used medicinally to slow and calm the mind,
has a higher yield than Sativa, used medicinally to relieve
depression by speeding up and lightening the mind.
The leftover leaves and stems of *Cannabis indica* can
make gorgeous shades of light, mellow yellows and
glowing greens.

1 NM	2 AL
3 AL+FE	4 FE

Juniper Berries

—

Juniperus communis L.

Juniper berries are the main flavoring agent in gin, whose
name comes from the Dutch and French names for juniper.
Junipers are evergreens, and their "berries" are female
seed cones. Juniper has been used extensively as a spice
in Scandinavia, Germany, and the Alsace region of France.
In Western folklore juniper was said to ward off witches
and evil spirits, and in Eastern folklore that it protected
against the "evil eye"; Tibetans believed it to ward
off demons. Harvested in the fall, juniper berries make
a wonderfully pungent spice. The warm yellow and ocher
tones of juniper relax and ground our senses.

1 NM	2 AL
3 AL+FE	4 FE

Absinthe

—

Artemisia absinthium

Artemisia absinthium, commonly known as absinthe or wormwood, is native to the temperate regions of Eurasia and Northern Africa. It holds a special place in multiple cultures, as it is known as the key ingredient in the infamous spirit absinthe as well as other alcoholic beverages, including bitters, Pelinkovac, and vermouth. Wormwood has featured in centuries of culturally rich storytelling. *Artemisia absinthium* is easily grown in arid soils and is naturalized in many areas of North America and in the Kashmir Valley of India. The colors extracted from *Artemisia absinthium* range from warm yellows to spirited golds and complex, nuanced golden-greens.

1 NM	2 AL
3 AL+FE	4 FE

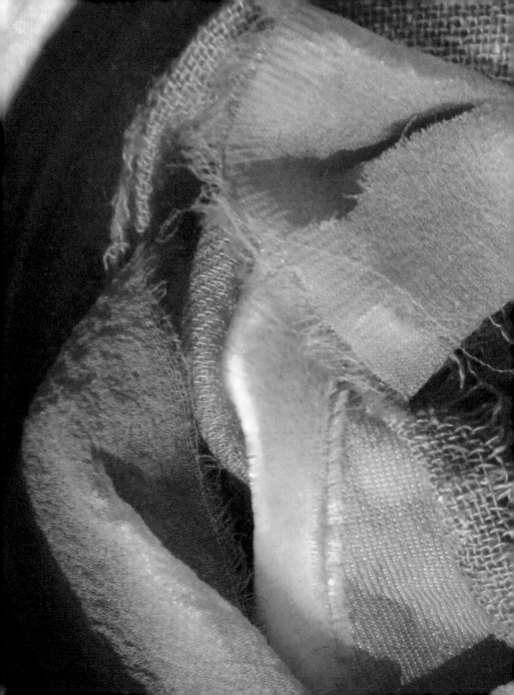

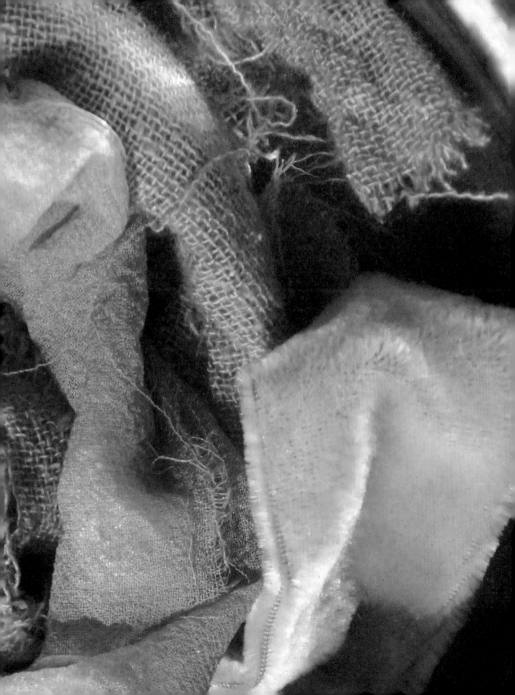

22   PALETTE CLEANSE

Red Cabbage   Red Banana Peels   Asparagus

Detox your color with this palette made from the by-products of antioxidant-boosting and cleansing foods. Vital, healthy yellows from turmeric and palette-cleansing pastels from asparagus greens, red cabbage, and grapefruit peels create a fresh palette of highly vibrational and medicinally beneficial hues.

Grapefruit Peels   Turmeric Root

Red Cabbage

—

Brassica oleracea

Red cabbage was known to the ancient Romans as a medicinal cure-all. It is most stable as a colorant on protein fibers. The depth and beauty of this health-restoring palette is worth your care. Boiled red cabbage can be strained and the water reused for pinks, blues, purples, and greens, depending upon the pH.

1 NM	2 AL
3 AL+FE	4 FE

Red Banana Peels

—

Musa acuminata

Red bananas, with their distinctive red and purple peels, have more vitamin C and higher beta carotene levels than the Cavendish banana, the common yellow cultivar familiar from any grocery store. The redder the banana peel, the higher the vitamin C. Bananas are by far the most popular fruit in the world, and banana trees are some of the fastest growing. Banana bunches come from a single flower bloom; one bunch can weigh as much as fifty pounds. Both red and yellow bananas can produce great compost colors, offering slightly different shades. Yellow bananas create natural hues, from beige to soft ecru yellows to greenish grays and rich charcoal blacks, while red bananas display a variety of colors, ranging from light mauves to rich pinks to inky grays.

1 NM	2 AL
3 AL+FE	4 FE

Asparagus

—

Asparagus officinalis

The water from steamed asparagus, as well as the leafy fronds of any garden-grown asparagus gone to seed, can be reused to create subtle, glowing yellows and greens. Asparagus is an herbaceous perennial native to the western coasts of Europe—from Ireland and Great Britain to the north of Spain and Germany. Dating back to nearly 3000 BCE, it was used as an offering in ancient Egyptian religious ceremonies. Asparagus has long been used as both a vegetable and a medicine and was prized by the Greeks and Romans for its cleansing properties. Typically, the young shoots of asparagus are what is eaten; when not harvested, the plant can quickly go to seed, making the stalk quite woody. With its various shades of glowing greens, asparagus is good for both your diet and your dye pot.

1	2
NM	AL
3	4
AL+FE	FE

Grapefruit Peels

—

Citrus x *paradisi*

Grapefruit, super high in vitamin C, is wonderful for boosting the immune system, calming to the nervous system, and great for digestion. It holds more water than almost any other fruit, at 92 percent. Grapefruit delivers a lot of nutrition for its small number of calories, making it a top fruit for cleansing. Reusing grapefruit peels, saved after eating or juicing, is an excellent way of making gorgeous yellow and light green shades.

1 NM	2 AL
3 AL+FE	4 FE

Turmeric Root

—

Curcuma longa

Turmeric is a powerful tropical root that is rich in antioxidants and anti-inflammatories and potent as a natural dye. Turmeric has been used in Asia as a medicine and a dye for thousands of years. It is an integral part of traditional Chinese medicine as well as the Indian practices of Ayurvedic, Siddha, and Unani medicine. Curcumin, found in turmeric root, can help to heal scars and skin wounds. Turmeric remains an accessible medicinal hue, healthy and easy to work with. That same vitality in a turmeric latte can also refresh a favorite dress again and again—offering perhaps the ultimate natural color cleanse for you and your wardrobe. The colors made from turmeric root range from bright yellows to deep orange and light to dark, greenish ochers.

1	2
NM	AL
3	4
AL+FE	FE

Color Therapy

Many medicinal plants in Western herbalism
can be noted for their color, including calendula,
nettles, and yarrow, among many others. Indigo
has also long been prized both for its dark
blue hues and for its medicinal qualities. Many
of the most light and colorful natural dyes
we know today are also used as medicinal herbs
in Ayurvedic practices as well as in traditional
Chinese medicine.

Turmeric, for instance, is known for its
application as a medicine to help with skin inflammation and irritation. It also produces a very
bright, even florescent, yellow dye, without any
additional mordant added. When used as a dye or
a colorant, its color eventually fades to a lighter
version through wear, light, and wash; reapplying
the color can be healing both during the process
of dyeing and when you wear it, as it is absorbed
into the largest organ of your body—your skin.
As a natural color, turmeric is healthy and easy to
refresh. There are many other medicinal natural

dye plants that have the potential to be soothing, healing for your skin, beneficial to circulation, or even useful when applied topically as a poultice—very different from working with synthetic chemicals. Working with plant-based dyes and deepening our understanding of their healing potential and properties gives the notion of "color therapy" a much deeper meaning.

23 HEALING HUES

Cutch   Himalayan Rhubarb Root   Kamala

In both Ayurveda, an ancient system of holistic wellness rooted in India, and traditional Chinese medicine, these special dye plants hold elevated positions due to their healing capacities. The plants in this palette have not only been used as colors for thousands of years but also hold important medicinal qualities. The healing hues shown in this palette are all made without additional added mordants to achieve the purest color possible.

Myrobalan   Tulsi

Cutch

—

Acacia catechu

Made from the wood of several species of acacia trees, most especially *Acacia catechu*, cutch is a colorant that creates deep reddish browns. Cutch has been used since ancient times as an astringent in Ayurvedic medicine as well as an everyday breath freshener, and was added to licorice pastilles and liquors in Italy and France. Conjuring the sweet flavor notes of maple syrup when brewed, this dye brings dark, warm richness to the palette. Loaded with tannins, cutch has also been used as a tanning agent and as a protectant for ropes and sails. Cutch creates warm browns on silk and wools, yellow browns on vegetable fibers, and deep gray-browns when iron is added.

1 NM	2 AL
3 AL+FE	4 FE

Himalayan Rhubarb Root

—

Rheum emodi

A powerful digestive, Himalayan rhubarb root is one
of the most widely used herbs in Chinese medicine.
The root is also proven as an external treatment for burns
and for soothing the skin. It grows well in higher slopes
and elevations and is native to the mountains of India,
Nepal, and China. A bright yellow and an orange dye can
be achieved from the root, depending on concentration,
and with iron added produces beautiful greens and ochers.

1	2
NM	AL
3	4
AL+FE	FE

Kamala

—

Mallotus philippensis

Kamala is a medicinal plant used in Ayurvedic and other practices. It grows in tropical India and is widely used as a traditional medicine throughout Asia. All parts of the kamala tree can be applied externally to fight skin parasites. Kamala color is made from the glandular hairs that grown on the outside of the kamala fruit. Kamala works best as a dye on protein fibers like wool and silk and in alkaline water; it provides peachy yellows, ochery oranges, olive, and khaki.

1 NM	2 AL
3 AL+FE	4 FE

Myrobalan

—

Terminalia chebula

Myrobalan is a strong dye made from the ground nuts of the *Terminalia chebula* tree, which grows in Nepal, India, Sri Lanka, Southeast Asia, and southern China. Myrobalan is an important dye and mordant, as the strength of its tannins can help to stabilize other dyes on a variety of fibers.

1 NM	2 AL
3 AL+FE	4 FE

Tulsi

—

Ocimum sanctum

Tulsi, also known as holy basil, is considered an herb for all purposes in Ayurvedic medicine. An aromatic shrub in the basil family, tulsi originated in north-central Asia and then spread through the tropics of the Eastern Hemisphere. It is an antimicrobial, a mosquito repellent, and an anti-inflammatory, among many other benefits rooted in its ability to defend the body against toxins. Tulsi produces sandy and golden yellows as well as deeper greens.

1 NM	2 AL
3 AL+FE	4 FE

24   HERBAL HUES

Culinary Sage   Lavender   Mint

Create a color story harvested directly from your herb garden. Herbs, valued since ancient times, engage multiple senses as they fulfill vital aromatic, medicinal, and culinary functions. These soothing greens made from lavender, mint, rosemary, sage, and thyme provide us with flavorful and evocative palettes imbued with herbal notes.

Rosemary   Thyme

Culinary Sage

—

Salvia officinalis

The largest genus in the mint family, *Salvia* comprises many varietals of sage plants that provide beautiful plant-made color palettes. Cultivated throughout the world, sage has a very long history of both culinary and medicinal uses. In ancient times, it was commonly used to ward off evil, and many still use it today in cleansing and purifying rituals. The sage used in this palette is known as culinary, garden, or common sage. Culinary sage creates strong, bold yellows as well as rich and dark greens.

1	2
NM	AL
3	4
AL+FE	FE

Lavender

—

Lavandula

Lavender is a flowering plant in the mint family. Native
to North Africa and the Mediterranean, it loves temperate
climates and is very drought tolerant. Lavender is used
as an ornamental in landscaping and as a culinary herb as
well as a perfume element and a medicinal essential oil.
English lavender is most commonly used in cooking,
its sweet, aromatic fragrance holding a range of delightful
citrus notes. The greens of lavender have a similar profile
to rosemary and can be used on their own for memorable
flavors. Lavender produces colors from light tans to
yellows, from greens to purple-grays, depending on
both the variety and the pH of the water.

1 NM	2 AL
3 AL+FE	4 FE

Mint

—

Mentha x *piperita*

All mints can create beautiful colors—typically yellows
but also minty greens to dark grays. The colors here were
extracted from chocolate mint, a variety that grows well
in the sun. Chocolate mint is a hybrid of water mint and
spearmint and is especially fun to grow in your herb garden
for its slightly chocolaty flavor. Mint is an excellent candidate for natural dyeing due to its prolific, weedy nature
in the garden and how readily it can be found in the wild.
Undomesticated mint can often be found in habitats
with moisture such as drainage areas and creek-side beds.
Mint can help with a number of health issues, including
tummy troubles (when used as a tea) or itching and muscle
or nerve pain (when used topically). Mint leaves, stems,
and roots conjure pastel yellows, greens, and grays.

1	2
NM	AL
3	4
AL+FE	FE

Rosemary

—

Rosmarinus officinalis

A woody perennial herb, rosemary is native to both
Asia and the Mediterranean. In some areas of the world,
rosemary is an invasive species. It is very drought tolerant
and therefore great for xeriscaping. It is also pest resistant and can prevent topical infections. The plant has
long been considered conducive to memory and is said
to help active thought and recall; it was used as a symbol
of remembrance in Elizabethan England at weddings
and funerals. Rosemary, in addition to being an herbal
flavoring, is used in incense, perfumes, shampoos, and
cleaning products. The color palettes made from rosemary
branches and leaves range from tans and yellows to
greens, teals, and grays.

1	2
NM	AL
3	4
AL+FE	FE

Thyme

—

Thymus vulgaris

The flowers and leaves of thyme have long been known
for their antifungal, antiseptic, and insecticidal properties.
Thyme was used in ancient Greece as a purifying incense,
and in Egypt to embalm. It has also been used to treat
respiratory diseases and conditions. Thyme creates warm
light golden yellows, celadon greens, and rich green-grays.

1 NM	2 AL
3 AL+FE	4 FE

25 COLOR MEDICINE

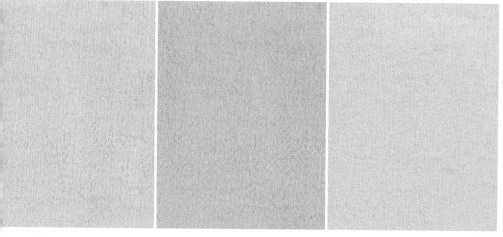

Slippery Elm Bark

Aloe Leaves

Calendula Flowers

Soothing shades from calendula, calming pinks from aloe leaves, and restorative greens from comfrey— these plant dyes offer healing remedies and beautiful color. Good for improving the skin as well as boosting immunity, these therapeutic tones from medicinal plants make gorgeous, healthy hues.

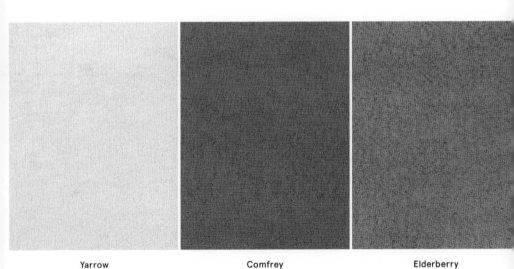

Yarrow   Comfrey   Elderberry

Slippery Elm Bark

—

Ulmus rubra

Soothing slippery elm bark is a remedy for a variety of ailments, including fevers, sore throats, and—when used topically—skin irritations, psoriasis, and wounds. A tree native to the central and eastern parts of the United States and into Ontario, its healing properties have been used and valued by Native Americans for centuries. The colors made from slippery elm bark range from pretty light pinks to dusty mauves and grays.

1 NM	2 AL
3 AL+FE	4 FE

Aloe Leaves

—

Aloe

Aloe is a succulent whose soothing plant gel helps to heal, to hydrate and protect the skin from the sun's powerful UV rays. The aloe plant can also make calming colors. It is used as a plant dye in many areas of South Africa, where its roots are most often used to dye wool red and brown. From the leaves, you can make luminous, soft yellows and pinks without the use of any additional mordant.

1	2
NM	AL
3	4
AL+FE	FE

Calendula Flowers

—

Calendula

High in flavonoids (compounds found in plants, believed
to have antimicrobial and antioxidant properties),
calendula has been shown to speed the healing of wounds
and to be immensely soothing to the skin. It can help
to salve rope burns, sunburns, cuts, and bruises, and
it is a treatment for eczema. Calendula can also be added
to a bath to improve circulation. Calendula, in the daisy
family, is easy to grow. In the dye bath, it yields beautiful,
soft, glowing yellows and greens.

1 NM	2 AL
3 AL+FE	4 FE

Yarrow

—

Achillea millefolium

Yarrow is a powerful plant with deep healing abilities, especially when used topically on the skin. It is also known to help with both blood clotting and circulation. Golden yarrow is a great plant to cultivate in a coastal garden, as it is highly attractive to native pollinators, especially butterflies. Yarrow creates gorgeous natural dye colors, from light to bright yellows and light to dark greens.

1	2
NM	AL
3	4
AL+FE	FE

Comfrey

—

Symphytum officinale L.

Known as a "bone knitter," comfrey can also be used as a poultice and applied directly to the skin. As a dye, the plant produces a light yellow-green with no mordant. For treating acne and psoriasis, comfrey is very helpful, as both the leaves and flowers have powerful anti-inflammatory properties. Comfrey creates colors from ochers to rich dark greens.

1 NM	2 AL
3 AL+FE	4 FE

Elderberry

—

Sambucus

Elderberries are known in the ancient lore of folk medicine for their prolific healing properties. With their powerful antioxidants, elderberries can boost the immune system, and the berries are deeply healing as a natural detoxifying agent when applied as a poultice. Elderberry colors are pH sensitive—thus, how the colors are modified, what water is used, and the soil the tree grew in can all make a difference. This elderberry palette ranges from purply mauves (with no mordant added) to rich, earthy charcoals (with iron added).

1 NM	2 AL
3 AL+FE	4 FE

Afterword

Working with natural color can support and deepen cultural, social, and environmental connections. This process helps us to make smart, visually dynamic, and meaningful choices; to decrease our carbon footprint; to connect with local, seasonal ingredients; and to repurpose food and green waste. The future of natural color lies in understanding the immense potential of plant-based palettes to increase biodiversity, care for ecosystems, and bring health and balance to our current unsustainable system based on profit over people and planet. Plants and their interdependencies can also help guide us to new regenerative models and teach us how to balance and shift our systems accordingly to nourish both nature AND culture—as well as to assess what makes sense over time.

Our material culture is being called to detox. Over 70 percent of homewares and textiles produced today are made using synthetic chemicals, and 17 to 20 percent of industrial water pollution is from dyeing and finishing treatments of textiles. The fast-fashion industry is the second-dirtiest industry, after only Big Oil.

According to the EPA, just since the 1960s, textile waste has increased by 811 percent in the United States. Reassessing our material culture by consuming consciously—and radically less—has an undeniable impact on our health and environment. We can begin to appreciate the myriad advantages of plant-based palettes—from their ecological benefits to the immense potential of herbal and healing hues that take us to new levels of holistic practices to the creative promise of ever-more personalized and naturally conceptual color choices. Just as sustainable food systems are an investment in our vitality and health, alternatives to mass produced fast-fashion and textiles are also essential.

Participation is the key to a more vitally rich and colorful future—from better understanding and caring for our ecologies to repurposing food and green waste in our communities and homes to knowing and growing climate-beneficial plants to creating gardens and agricultural systems that support pollinators and local, organic flora and food systems. Nature teaches us when to evolve and rebalance. Natural palettes can add depth and circular connectivity to the creative process: nourishing the seeds of plant-made spectra to come and allowing us to learn and collaborate intrinsically and holistically, designing as nature does, with zero waste, regenerative purpose, and undeniable beauty.

Acknowledgments

To my family: thank you for nourishing me to plant these seeds and harvest these hues. Scott: I am ever grateful for your love, creative vision, ecological wisdom, and endless editing. Thank you for helping me to truly see a vibrant future and for sharing it with me in the present every day. To Bergamot, Beckett, and Finn: I will never know better teachers of wonder, assistants of awe, and foraging companions in these plant-based color fields—I love you! To my awe-inspiring Mom and Dad: you are always my true-hued inspiration from the beginning and forever. Thank you for letting me play in all those puddles—love you both oceans. To my wonderful siblings, Lissa, Cael, Kit, and Martha: thank you for playing in those puddles with me—and for all the creativity, humor, and support and for Ohana Dinners to Dye For in our very near future. To the generations above and to the ones upcoming: my heartfelt appreciation for you all—thank you for being my muses and my motivation.

To my agent, Lindsay Edgecombe: I am deeply grateful for your support of this book and concept from its very beginning and for your strong belief in the importance of living color. I am so lucky to have you—as both my advocate and as a friend.

My sincere thanks and appreciation to Monica LoCascio for your talent and supreme visual design abilities in showcasing how this book could look in our initial proposal.

To my amazing team at Princeton Architectural Press: I am infinitely appreciative to have been paired with such a talented and kind team. So much gratitude to my wonderful editor, Rob Shaeffer, for supporting and believing in the power of plant-made palettes and all their potential. Thank you for your guidance, encouragement, shared perspective—and all our creatively engaging conversations on art and life. To my art director, Paul Wagner: your aesthetic and visual talent are essential to this book on plants and color—my deepest thanks for all you do. To my project editor, Sara Stemen: my sincere gratitude for helping me to refine these concepts and for your expertise in helping to make these words and ideas shine.

To Katelyn Toth-Fejel and Deepa Natarajan: thank you for all your early and hard work with me on concepts around Permacouture systems and practices—I am forever grateful to what came out of those early years—and for working with natural color both as a social practice and as an environmental inquiry through process and care. To my Slow Fashion and Textile colleagues, especially to Lynda Grose and Kate Fletcher: thank you for your inspiration in imagining all the diversity and biodiversity of ways. To the Textiles program at California College of the Arts: thank you for believing in me and for believing in the important intersection that natural color, slow food, and slow textiles bring to true change in curriculum and deeper connections in the world, and always with appreciation and gratitude to my mentors, Deborah Valoma and Lia Cook, for supporting this work from the start. To Susanne Cockrell: thank you, my friend, for your dedication, sense of humor, and belief in honoring place-based connections; thank you for seeing the vision and planting the first seeds in the garden with me. For my true-hued friend, Abigail Doan: your inspiration, guidance, and vision of environmental togetherness is always a guiding light and tactile truth. I am ever grateful for your kinship on this walking journey. So much love to Casey Larkin for your natural color collaborations, humor and support, and for foraging for fashion (forever). For my slow-food friends and advocates, especially to Amanda Rieux and Lissa Duerr for working with me at the Edible Schoolyard for two years, and to Kelsie Kerr: thank you for your wisdom and collaboration, and support of ecoliteracy and biodiversity through creativity in taste and palettes.

To my natural-color creative community, colleagues, students, and friends: I am blessed to have the depth of support, encouragement, conversations, and collaborations over all these years. Thank you for making my world more colorful—and for sharing and celebrating the wonder.

My deepest gratitude and love for the generations of people on all reaches of this planet that have cared for and kept biodiversity, ecologies, and plant-based color alive. Thank you.

Further Reading

Aftel, Mandy. *Fragrant: The Secret Life of Scent*. New York: Riverhead Books, 2014.

Albers, Josef. *Interaction of Color*. 50th Anniversary Edition. New Haven, CT: Yale University Press, 2013.

Anderson, M. Kat. *Tending the Wild: Native American Knowledge and the Management of California's Natural Resources*. Berkeley: University of California Press, 2006.

Ashworth, Suzanne. *Seed to Seed: Seed Saving and Growing Techniques for Vegetable Gardeners*. Decorah, IA: Seed Savers Exchange, 2002.

Bittner, Stefani, and Alethea Harampolis. *Harvest: Unexpected Projects Using 47 Extraordinary Garden Plants*. Berkeley, CA: Ten Speed Press, 2017.

Blankenship, Jana. *Wild Beauty: Wisdom and Recipes for Natural Self-Care*. Berkeley, CA: Ten Speed Press, 2019.

Bliss, Anne. *Weeds: A Guide for Dyers and Herbalists*. Boulder, CO: Juniper House, 1978.

Booth, Abigail. *The Wild Dyer: A Maker's Guide to Natural Dyes with Projects to Create and Stitch*. New York: Princeton Architectural Press, 2019.

Boutrup, Joy, and Catherine Ellis. *The Art and Science of Natural Dyes: Principles, Experiments and Results*. Atglen, PA: Schiffer, 2019.

Buchanan, Rita. *A Dyer's Garden: From Plant to Pot, Growing Dyes for Natural Fibers*. Fort Collins, CO: Interweave Press, 1995.

Burgess, Rebecca. *Harvesting Color: How to Find Plants and Make Natural Dyes*. New York: Artisan, 2011.

Cardon, Dominique. *Natural Dyes*. Suffolk, UK: Antique Collectors Club, 2007.

Carson, Rachel. *Silent Spring*. Anniversary Edition. Boston: Houghton Mifflin, 2002.

Cline, Elizabeth. *Overdressed: The Shockingly High Cost of Fast Fashion*. New York: Penguin, 2012.

Coles, David. *Chromotopia: An Illustrated History of Color*. London: Thames and Hudson, 2019.

Dean, Jenny. *Wild Color: The Complete Guide to Making and Using Natural Dyes*. Rev. ed. New York: Potter Craft, 2010.

Desnos, Rebecca. *Botanical Colour at Your Fingertips*. UK: Self-published, 2018.

Duerr, Sasha. *The Handbook of Natural Plant Dyes: Personalize Your Craft with Organic Colors from Acorns, Blackberries, Coffee, and Other Everyday Ingredients*. Portland, OR: Timber Press, 2011.

———. *Natural Color: Vibrant Plant Dye Projects for Your Home and Wardrobe*. New York: Watson-Guptill, 2016.

Eiseman, Leatrice, and Keith Recker. *Pantone: The Twentieth Century in Color*. San Francisco: Chronicle Books, 2011.

Fletcher, Kate. *Craft of Use: Post-Growth Fashion*. Abingdon, UK: Routledge, 2016.

———. *Sustainable Fashion and Textiles: Design Journeys*. London: Earthscan, 2008.

———. *Wild Dress: Clothing and the Natural World*. Devon, UK: Uniform Books, 2019.

Fletcher, Kate, and Lynda Grose. *Fashion and Sustainability: Design for Change*. London: Laurence King, 2012.

Flint, India. *Eco Colour: Botanical Dyes for Beautiful Textiles*. Fort Collins, CO: Interweave Press, 2010.

———. *Second Skin: Choosing and Caring for Textiles and Clothing*. Sydney: Murdoch Books, 2012.

Gladstar, Rosemary. *Rosemary Gladstar's Medicinal Herbs: A Beginner's Guide: 33 Healing Herbs to Know, Grow, and Use*. North Adams, MA: Storey Publishing, 2012.

Holmgren, David. *Permaculture: Principles and Pathways Beyond Sustainability*. Hepburn Springs, Australia: Holmgren Design Services, 2017.

Kimmerer, Robin Wall. *Braiding Sweetgrass: Indigenous Wisdom, Scientific Knowledge, and the Teachings of Plants.* Minneapolis: Milkweed Editions, 2015.

Krohn-Ching, Val. *Hawaii Dye Plants and Dye Recipes.* Honolulu: University of Hawaii Press, 2016.

Lewis, Sarah Wyndham. *Planting for Honeybees: The Grower's Guide to Creating a Buzz.* London: Quadrille, 2018.

Logan, Jason. *Make Ink: A Forager's Guide to Natural Inkmaking.* New York: Abrams, 2018.

Lonsdale, Sarah, and Louesa Roebuck. *Foraged Flora: A Year of Gathering and Arranging Wild Plants and Flowers.* Berkeley, CA: Ten Speed Press, 2016.

Natarajan, Deepa Preeti, and Helen Krayenhoff. *10 Plants for Color: A Simple Guide to Growing and Using Natural Dye Plants.* Berkeley, CA: Self-published, 2017.

Orr, David. *Ecological Literacy: Educating Our Children for A Sustainable World.* San Francisco: Sierra Club Books, 2005.

Pamer, Kerilynn, and Cindy Diprima Morisse. *High Vibrational Beauty: Recipes & Rituals for Radical Self Care.* New York: Rodale Books, 2018.

Pate, Maggie. *The Natural Colors Cookbook: Custom Hues for your Fabrics Made Simple Using Food.* Boston: Page Street, 2018.

Plevin, Julia. *The Healing Magic of Forest Bathing: Finding Calm, Creativity, and Connection in the Natural World.* Berkeley, CA: Ten Speed Press, 2019.

Pursell, J. J. *The Herbal Apothecary: 100 Herbs and How to Use Them.* Portland, OR: Timber Press, 2015.

Raichur, Pratima. *Absolute Beauty: Radiant Skin and Inner Harmony Through the Ancient Secrets of Ayurveda.* New York: William Morrow Paperbacks, 1999.

Recker, Keith. *True Colors: World Masters of Natural Dyes and Pigments.* Loveland, CO: Thurms Books, 2019.

Redzepi, René, and Daniel Zilber. *The Noma Guide to Fermentation.* New York: Artisan, 2018.

Refslund, Mads, and Tama Matsuoka Wong. *Scraps, Wilt & Weeds: Turning Wasted Food into Plenty*. New York: Grand Central Life & Style, 2017.

Reid, Georgina. *The Planthunter: Truth, Beauty, Chaos, and Plants*. Portland, OR: Timber Press, 2019.

Richards, Lynne. Tyrl, *Ronald J. Dyes from American Native Plants: A Practical Guide* Portland, OR: Timber Press. 2005.

Rodabaugh, Katrina. *Mending Matters*. New York: Abrams, 2018.

Royal Botanical Gardens Kew and Jason Irving. *The Gardener's Companion to Medicinal Plants: An A-Z of Healing Plants and Home Remedies*. London: Frances Lincoln, 2017.

St. Clair, Kassia. *The Secret Lives of Color*. New York: Penguin, 2016.

Stewart, Amy. *The Drunken Botanist: The Plants that Create the World's Great Drinks*. Chapel Hill, NC: Algonquin, 2013.

Studio Nienke Hoogvliet. *Seaweed Research*. The Hague, Netherlands: Self-published, 2017.

Tanov, Erica. *Design by Nature: Creating Layered, Lived-In Spaces Inspired by the Natural World*. Berkeley, CA: Ten Speed Press, 2018.

Trinder, Kingston. *An Atlas of Rare & Familiar Colour: The Harvard Art Museums' Forbes Pigment Collection*. Los Angeles: Atelier Editions, 2018.

Vejar, Kristine. *The Modern Natural Dyer: A Comprehensive Guide to Dyeing Silk, Wool, Linen, and Cotton at Home*. New York: Stewart, Tabori & Chang, 2015.

Wada, Sanzo. *A Dictionary Of Color Combinations*. Kyoto, Japan: Seingesha, 2011.

Waters, Alice, Kelsie Kerr, Patricia Curtan, and Fritz Streiff. *The Art of Simple Food: Notes, Lessons, and Recipes from a Delicious Revolution*. New York: Clarkson Potter, 2007.

Yamazaki, Seiju. *The Illustrated Book of Dye Plants*. Tokyo: Bijutsu Shuppan-Sha, 1996.

Index of Plants

LATIN NAMES

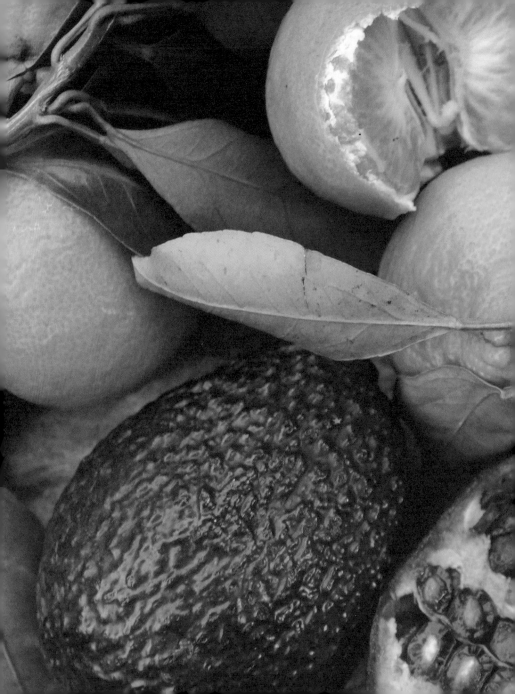

Published by
Princeton Architectural Press
70 West 36th Street
New York, New York 10018
www.papress.com

Editor: Sara Stemen
Designer: Paul Wagner

Library of Congress Cataloging-in-Publication Data
    Names: Duerr, Sasha, author.
Title: Natural palettes : inspiration from plant-based color /
    Sasha Duerr.
Description: First edition. | New York : Princeton Architectural
    Press, [2020] | Includes bibliographical references. | Summary:
    "An innovative plant-based color guide that includes twenty-
    five palettes with five hundred natural color swatches,
    providing inspiration for sustainable fashion, textiles, fine art,
    floral design, food, medicine, gardening, interior design, and
    other creative disciplines"—Provided by publisher.
Identifiers: LCCN 2019024084 (print) | LCCN 2019024085 (ebook) |
    ISBN 9781616897925 (paperback) | ISBN 9781616897925 (epub)
Subjects: LCSH: Color in design. | Dye plants.
Classification: LCC NK1548 .D84 2020 (print) | LCC NK1548
    (ebook) | DDC 701/.85—dc23
LC record available at https://lccn.loc.gov/2019024084
LC ebook record available at https://lccn.loc.gov/2019024085